D1225162

ART OF THE WESTERN WORLD

VENETIAN PAINTING

MARCO VALSECCHI

GOLDEN PRESS NEW YORK

ART OF THE WESTERN WORLD

General Editor Marco Valsecchi

VENETIAN PAINTING

Translated from the Italian by Pearl Sanders

Published in the U.S.A. by Golden Press, Inc.,
New York.

The paintings reproduced in this book were photographed by Studio Scala

Printed in Italy Istituto Geografico De Agostini S. p. A. - Novara 1962

INTRODUCTION

The progress of Venetian art is like that of a great river, flowing uninterruptedly across a landscape of six centuries. In each decade, as if by a miracle, its impulse is renewed by the inpouring of fresh talent and genius. The art of Venice lasted the longest of any region of Italy, longer even than the art of Tuscany, to which at various times, however, it was considerably indebted.

The reason for this long and flourishing period of art is perhaps to be found in the free artistic atmosphere of Venice. Venetian art did not keep jealously to itself; on the contrary, it always sought after exchanges and contacts with the outside, and by welcoming men and ideas from other parts, it was itself continually renewed. This can be seen by a glance at Venice of the late sixteenth century. For a time after the death of the great masters, Titian, Veronese, Bassano, and Tintoretto, the Venetian scene remained deserted. The younger generation believed they could continue to live off the heritage left by their elders. But time moves on, the intellectual outlook changes, and civilisation, together with history, is in constant movement. Men cannot stop to worship the past, however glorious and splendid it may have been. Thus, the serious gap which the death of these great masters had left in Venetian art was in danger of remaining unfilled if the young men could not rouse themselves to renew their inspiration by fresh examples and ideas. But then once more, in the middle of the seventeenth century, a number of artists appeared from other parts of Italy: Liss, Feti, Strozzi; and in the ferment of activity which resulted from the stimulus of their new ideas, was born the happy era of the Venetian eighteenth century. Napoleon's drastic decision to end the existence of the Venetian Republic resulted in the loss of civil liberties and the extinguishing of artistic imagination. There remained Canova, an artist who had left Venice to work in Rome, to testify to that great period, especially with his youthful works which were close to the inspiration of the Baroque temperament. Then came a cold neo-Classical aestheticism which in a few years cooled even his fervour, and Venetian art declined into an inert academic formalism. Yet its course had been long, fruitful and generous, compassing six centuries, and of a splendour which has never been equalled.

The first name to emerge in the history of Venetian painting is that of Paolo Veneziano, in the first half of the fourteenth century; he was already a master, at least for his city. He cannot, it is true, be compared with Duccio of Siena, although they both have their roots in Byzantine art, and even less so with Giotto, who in the early years of the century had already painted the frescoes in the Arena Chapel in Padua, which were to inject new life into the whole of Italian art.

Yet Paolo himself was not the first artist to appear on the Venetian scene. Although they are now reduced to pale images or battered fragments, we cannot ignore the fresco remains in the Cathedral of Adria, in the Concordia Baptistery, all painted about the year 1000, or the fragment, of possibly earlier date, in Torcello; and above all the two fresco cycles in the Basilica of Aquileia. In the apse fresco, painted in 1031, the Emperor Corrado appears with the Empress Gisella and their son Corrado. In the second cycle, which decorate the crypt, there are, among other episodes, scenes from the Passion, which date from about 1200.

In these last frescoes, we have a style of painting which has been handed down by Byzantine art. But the immediateness and dramatic vigour of these frescoes is highly expressive, and we see in them for the first time the cold, impassive style of Byzantine art forced, as it were, to adapt itself to a new and warmer climate. For this reason, some scholars, while admitting the growing penetration of Byzantine forms, ask whether such frescoes as those of Aquileia might not be a much livelier and typically Italian adaptation of the traditional modes of Byzantine art.

By the side of the frescoes of the neighbouring mainland should be placed those painted in Venice itself, as examples of a style frequently to be found in the Laguna. The fragments in San Niccolò di Lido were destroyed in the war, but recently other thirteenth century frescoes have been discovered in San Zan Degolà, which are very different in feeling from the Aquileian frescoes. Then there were the influences of Paduan art, which spread by means of miniatures in sacred books, and a Romanesque cursive style, not at all Byzantine, is to be found in the timber house where the body of Beata Giuliana was brought after her death in 1622. These remarks are merely to show that Venetian art was not formed all at once, nor was it the result only of the Byzantine art brought over from the east; for although Byzantine art was prevalent in Venice, it was modified and often given much greater liveliness by local minor artists, whose work may have been unpolished but was also closer to popular instincts and of greater depth of feeling than was to be found in the lucid formal symbols of the courtly artists of Byzantium.

And finally, there are the mosaics which decorate the Basilica of St Mark's. Until a few decades ago, these mosaics were believed to have been the work of artists who had come to Venice direct from Byzantium, but modern research has shown that they are mainly the work of local groups of artists or groups from nearby Ravenna. These artists were Byzantine by tradition, yet they were in possession of an autonomous artistic language, which was formed by a combination of local art with the Romanesque art practised on the mainland, and these artists can be considered the mainspring of Venetian art. While Byzantine art, by its use of symbols and ideal images, transfigured reality into abstracted forms, the St Mark's mosaics more and more frequently depicted reality, especially those mosaics which decorate the portico of the Basilica, among which is even to be found a rustic scene. For the linear frontality of eastern art, the St Mark's mosaicists substituted plastic relief and a broader perspective. The figures move with great freedom through the architectonic space and the effect of illusion is increased. In oriental Byzantine art, the gold ground tends to annul any indication of space, but in these western mosaics it assumes a colouristic function, so adding to the effect of space.

The St Mark's mosaics were executed from the middle of the twelfth century to the end of the thirteenth. This work did not develop in only one direction during this long period, and did not keep to the rigidity of Byzantine art. We can therefore conclude today that these mosaics, begun perhaps by Greek artists or modelled on an eastern pattern, were more and more modified under the influence of local or Romanesque artists. These influences did not follow a precise chronological development, and within each period groups of mosaicists worked in a great variety of styles: from the mosaics of a most orthodox Byzantine style—the earliest *Apostles* in the apse—to those of the style of Ravenna—the *Pentecost* cupola, for example—and finally the more frankly Romanesque and naturalistic mosaics depicting *Episodes in the Life of Noah* in the portico of the Basilica.

Paolo Veneziano came from the multiform artistic background which had been developing through these decades, and though he may be called a Byzantine painter, we also bear in mind the local Romanesque variations just mentioned. And indeed, his first works, from the Murano altar-piece of 1310 to the Dignano altar-piece of 1321, have a liveliness of narration which derives from other sources than Byzantine art, although its roots are in Byzantium. Probably the artist had also studied Giotto's frescoes in Padua and Rimini; but he adapted their teaching to his own method, although he certainly felt the attraction of the pomp and ritual of Byzantine art. The works which are closest to the oriental spirit, however, are those of his middle years, as we see from the *Death of the Virgin* in Vicenza, painted in 1333, where the most typical mannerisms of Byzantine art are adopted. We may therefore argue that the painter perhaps travelled to Constantinople, the capital of Byzantine art. Yet his Venetian origins and the complexity of his local artistic background were not entirely forgotten; they were to emerge again later, in the *Martyrdom of St Mark* (see Plate 1) which he began in 1343 and completed two years later. In this painting there is a much more obvious and lively narrative intent, the figures emerge from their Byzantine impassivity to enter a freer, and already architectonic, space. And finally, in the *Coronation of the Virgin* of 1358, now in the Frick Collection in New York, his painting is already influenced by Gothic art.

Gothic art did in fact reach Venice later than other parts of Italy. The Sienese painter, Simone Martini, was then dead (having died in Avignon in 1344), so that one of the most splendid and refined periods of Italian Gothic art had already ended by the time Paolo Veneziano first came under its influence. In these early centuries, Venice was slow to break away from its origins: and even when new art forms were accepted, they were soon absorbed into the Venetian background. The painting of Lorenzo Veneziano, who was a pupil of Paolo, was already clearly Gothic, as we can see from the *Lion Polyptych* of 1359 in Venice. There are no oriental profiles or threads of golden light in this work, and this is not owing to intellectual laziness, but to a conception of art which was to endure in Venetian painting: in particular, the primary importance of colour, which was to remain the constant foundation of Venetian painting, as opposed to the art of any other region.

The frequent and lively contacts maintained with Padua produced in Venice an ever more decidedly Gothic influence. This influence shows itself in the art of the rustic painter Guariento, as well as the more lyrical Altichiero or the more cultured and severe Tuscan, Giusto de Menabuoi. These years were indeed so fruitful for new forms of art that by the side of the Byzantine Basilica of St Mark's there rises the Gothic Ducal Palace. The new painters of the fourteenth and fifteenth centuries were all Gothic artists: Nicolò di Pietro, who on his travels reached even as far as Bohemia, Jacobello del Fiore, whose figures seem to flutter like the stone angels on the summit of St Mark's, and Giambono, whose rich and luscious paintings were all so glowing with life that the linear modelling was soon replaced by a blaze of colour, and henceforth the decorative function of colour was to take precedence over linearity. Venice was so closely connected with the mainland, that as its political and commercial fortunes expanded, so there arrived more and more artists from the mainland, who became widely acclaimed. Among these artists, Gentile da Fabriano, who worked in Venice about the year 1410, summoned Pisanello to work with him in 1415, and in Pisanello Venice acquired an artist of great refinement and culture; while the local artist Jacopo Bellini accompanied him to Florence, from where he brought back new ideas which were to turn his thoughts towards humanism. And fifteen years later, Masolino da Panicale returned from Hungary.

But in the Mascoli Chapel in St Mark's, at the time of the mosaic decoration of 1430, events which were to have a revolutionary effect on the whole course of Venetian art were taking place. Two pictures depicting *Episodes of the Life of the Virgin* are signed 'Michele Giambono'; they are the work of a Gothic artist of 'international' taste. The other two pictures, the *Visitation* and the *Death of the Virgin*, are of an entirely different culture, and clearly belong to Renaissance art, both for their monumental and architectural quality, as well as for the dramatic sombreness of the figures. What could have been the cause of the departure of Venetian painting from Gothic art at that time?

Naturally, we cannot, nor should we, exclude the possibility that some artists, such as Antonio Vivarini and his brother-in-law Giovanni d'Alemagna, may have been able to develop by means of their own intuition some of the artistic forms provided by artists whose work was transitional between Gothic and Renaissance. The critic Roberto Longhi has attributed to Antonio Vivarini the same position in Venetian art as was occupied by Masolino in the art of Florence. He has also indicated a trend in painting the principal exponent of which was Francesco Squarcione, 'tailor and repairer,' who was a man of Renaissance tastes rather than a Renaissance painter, and who recognised and raised in his studio the young Mantegna.

Yet we cannot ignore the frequent arrivals in Venice of Tuscan artists, from Paolo Uccello who arrived in 1425 and stayed until after 1433; Andrea del Castagno who painted in the Chapel of St Tarasio in the Venetian Church of San Zaccaria; Filippo Lippi who in 1433 was already in Padua, soon to be followed by Donatello. And we know too that in 1433 Melozzo too spent a short time in Venice. The mosaics in the Mascoli Chapel have been ascribed to Paolo Uccello himself, to Andrea del Castagno, and even to Andrea Mantegna, who in 1454 married Giambellino's sister and spent some time in Venice. They have also sometimes been ascribed to Jacopo Bellini, who was already imbued with the new ideas after his journey to Florence, and proof for this has been sought in his drawings in the famous notebooks in London and Paris. Yet whoever the artist may have been, it is clear that we have already left the refined air of Gothic art. However, in spite of the many Tuscan artists who came to Venice to bring new forms to local art, it was Padua once more which was to lead the way to the highest and most original humanistic art. This came about because of the long period which Donatello spent in Padua as well as the early growth of Mantegna's genius (Plates 4,5).

These two names were to attract the most intelligent young men of the time: Donatello, with his bronzes executed for the altar of St Antony and for the equestrian statue of Gattamelata, and Mantegna, with his frescoes in the Church of the Eremitani. Among these young men was Carlo Crivelli (Plate 3) who by his very personal vision was to develop highly individual forms from Gothic art yet without rejecting it. There came also the two Bellinis, Gentile and Giovanni, the latter following his brother-in-law Mantegna so closely that he assumed the modes and figures of that artist for a period of about ten years. The polyptychs in the Carità Church in Venice, the *Crucifixion* in the Correr Museum, the *Agony in the Garden* in London, were almost repetitions of the same themes as they were carried out by Mantegna in the famous predella for San Zeno in Verona in 1459.

In Mantegna the Renaissance found heroic expression. The powerful relief of his painted figures vies with the controlled energy of antique statues, and his passion for classicism and archeological erudition found expression in the clusters of ancient ruins strewn over the crags and rocks of his paintings. Above all, Mantegna strove to create an ideal reconstruction of a world of classical beauty and harmony, not merely as an ornament of court life, but rather as the reflection of an intimate life ordered on the pattern of these ancient models. In Giovanni Bellini (Plates 6,7) this enthusiasm for classical reconstruction will be maintained, mitigated however by a greater feeling for the pictorial aspects of daily life which are, as it were, but a reflection of the spiritual light which softens the harshness of the dramatic episodes of the Passion, both in the drawing of the figures and the colour, subtly blended and luminous.

It was Giovanni Bellini too who during the whole course of the fifteenth century and a good part of the following century—he died in 1516—achieved the most radical transformations in Venetian painting. He passed through all the experiences of his time, and his surprisingly flexible intelligence was always bent on finding a full and profound accord between man, his ideals and his complex environment. Time and again he seized the highest artistic achievements of his time and incorporated them within Venetian painting, which was thereafter to bear the imprint of his irreplaceable personality. It was due to him that the most precious gifts of Byzantine and Gothic art filtered through the new painting: the nobility of Byzantium coupled with a Gothic gentleness of colour. From Padua he was to introduce the humanistic idealism of Mantegna; he followed the new concepts of Piero della Francesca and Antonello (Plates 8,9) on the use of colour as a means of achieving effects of perspective, in place of drawing and chiaroscuro as taught by the Florentines; and finally, he prepared the way to Giorgione's discovery of colour enhanced by light to reflect depth of feeling. All these achievements were the result of Bellini's poetical imagination. That is why there is no intellectual effort to be seen in his art.

By the side of Giovanni Bellini, an artist of a younger generation, Carpaccio (Plate 10) painted within the new spatial perspective now offered to Venetian painters. As the crowds move through his tales, his stories of saints and hermits, his lively imagination paints the details of their daily life with the same minuteness as in Flemish painting. His interest in these fragments seems to break up his compositions, which become like Chinese boxes whose riddle is unravelled little by little by the searching eye. But certain bizarre effects and some cruel details, such as the macabre remains of the Dragon's frightful meal in his *St George* in the Scuola degli Schiavoni, bear witness to a fantastic liberty of imagination within the bounds of an almost documentary seriousness, like that of a pedantic chronicler. We cannot say that the miniaturist's microcosm lessens the tension of Carpaccio's composition, nor should we lose from sight, in his richly fantastic stories, the stupendous revelation of landscape, with the clear depths of the horizons bathed in light, or his amazingly vigorous imagination.

After Giovanni Bellini, the characteristic of Venetian painting of the sixteenth century will be the importance it places on light and colour. A deep feeling of pagan harmony runs through the pictorial world of Giorgione (Plate 11). His life was short, for he died of the plague in 1510, but although he painted for little more than ten years, he left an indelible imprint on Venetian painting. His painting unites the grace of the spirit with the beauty of the natural world, and by his use of luminous colour he created subtle and evocative moods. The human figures appear immersed in light, which lovingly clothes them in a transparent glow, while the landscape ceases to be an inert background, but itself becomes palpitating with life, in mysterious relation to the human figures. His paintings have a calm rhythm, and seem to be suspended in the expectancy of a miracle, in the fluid air of a delicately modulated perspective.

Titian (Plates 12,13) was to bring to this harmonious spiritual life the breath of warmer, more full-blooded and sensual life. The tranquil tonal effects of Giorgione are given the potency of sumptuous colour spread in wide chromatic zones. Titian's paintings reveal a monumental vision of contrasting broad masses of light. In the *Assumption* of 1518 in the Frari Church, this vitality so inflames the atmosphere of the painting that it becomes like a lake of light. In the *Pesaro Screen* of 1526 the monumentality of the characters is added to by the vigorous chromatic effect.

Titian passed through a period of ' Roman mannerism ' after the manner of Michelangelo. It began soon after 1540 and lasted less than five years. It enabled him finally to break through the closed schemas of Renaissance form and to achieve new effects of luminosity combined with a warm colouring which sparkles with rapid, vibrant brushstrokes. In the last decade of his life, Titian's vision was realised by breaking up his huge masses with sparkling bursts of light. In *Lucretia and Tarquin*, painted around 1570, and now in Vienna, the struggle takes place in an atmosphere rendered dramatic by the lightning flashes themselves; and by this startling innovation, Titian was to open up new perspectives to the tragic fantasy of Rembrandt.

The pictorial invention of Tintoretto (Plates 15,16), on the other hand, is based on violent effects of light, on the play of shadows, crossed by swords of light rays like cataracts of luminous arrows which break up the whole composition, creating a fantastic, theatrical animation. The *Miracle of the Slave*, painted at the age of thirty, already realises to the full Tintoretto's new method of treating narrative. The play of shadows broken up by the light gives life to the gestures and the rapid serpentine movements of his characters. The colour is subdued, and in place of brilliant colouristic effects, nocturnal shadows increase the spatial perspective. As in a great Baroque theatre, Tintoretto uses a vast human chorus to create myths of a magical, almost phantasmagorical vision. A powerful dramatic vitality is unleashed in his paintings, together with depth of feeling.

A contemporary of Tintoretto was Veronese (Plates 17,18). Unlike Tintoretto, his 'manneristic' style inclined rather towards a vision inundated with the cold light of morning which colours even the shadows with a more subdued luminosity. Veronese too produced vast compositions, with vertical perspectives rising steeply towards the pale clouds and creating bold contrasts in the clear and transparent air, in contrast to the solemn classical Palladian architecture of the porches and the ample, sonorous ceilings. The world of Veronese is usually evoked in joyous accents, its splendours reflected in the natural spectacle of pure light and colour.

Although he worked in the provinces, Bassano (Plate 19) is also to be considered a Venetian painter, both because his paintings followed the sixteenth century pattern of the painting of the Laguna with its stress on values of light and colour, and for his own personal contribution to the evolution of 'manneristic' painting. This was freely interpreted by painters of the succeeding generation from whom was to be born the visionary genius of El Greco. Bassano's compositions are freely articulated within a space which is enlarged by diagonal thrusts of light; and at the same time the colour increases in intensity, following the impulse of his lyrical imagination.

His paintings often repeat the themes of the *Adoration of the Shepherds*, the *Flight into Egypt*, and the nocturnal departure of the Hebrews for the Promised Land with their utensils and droves of cattle. These themes provide the pretext for representing the peasant life of his province, the seasonal migrations, the nocturnal bivouacs with sheep squatting around the fires, or the large country kitchens glittering with copper and jugs. Yet we should not overlook in his rustic scenes the elegance of his colour, the refined use of light which appears in unexpected masses, or in wide surfaces which sparkle as if illuminated in the darkness; and by his bold use of light Bassano creates a vision of magical effect. Yet at the same time as he was creating works of such inventive imagination, Bassano presented the first realistic images of a proletarian world. These were to be the fore-runners of a long period of seventeenth-century painting, and are of such melancholy as can be found only in certain poems of Tasso.

Towards the end of the century, all these great masters died within fifteen years of each other, leaving Venetian art like a deserted stage, and so it was to remain for many decades. A living culture can be maintained not by repeating old ideas, but only by continually renewing them with fresh insight. Perhaps, during the first half of the seventeenth century, new life might have been infused into Venetian painting by Saraceni, who painted in a Venetian, Caravaggesque manner. But no sooner had he returned from Rome when he died, at an early age, leaving several unfinished works.

In fact great seventeenth-century paintings were produced not in Venice, but in Rome, and also, for the first thirty years of the century, in Milan. The empty Venetian scene became peopled by painters from outside Venice, who were however deeply aware of the pictorial values of Venetian art: the Dutch painter Liss, the Roman Feti, and above all the Genoese Strozzi, with the vital colouring of his scenic compositions which are of great strength, although always somewhat heavy. His painting of *St Sebastian* for the Church of San Benedetto abounds in rhetoric, but through it there pounds a vital blood, if not exactly new ideas; and it was new blood of which Venetian painting had most need.

In the second half of the century again, foreign artists were most to the forefront. Some sent their paintings to Venice, others came themselves. They included Solimena of Naples, Cortona and Luca Giordano, and the intelligent and lively Florentine Sebastiano Mazzoni, who remained in Venice for many years, until his death in 1685. From Vicenza came Maffei, a Baroque painter whose bold brushstrokes dart like daggers full of ironic thrusts at the puffed up figures of the century. At the end of the century, the first landscape painters, Marco Ricci and especially Carlevari

Plate 1. PAOLO VENEZIANO:
The Martyrdom of St Mark (section of polyptych). Venice, Cathedral Museum.

who paved the way to Canaletto and his nephew, Bernardo Bellotto, took up the refrain, now in a minor key. Their paintings were less weighed down by rhetoric or academic culture, and were therefore of a more sparkling gaiety. These painters were the faithful chroniclers of the life of this beautiful city, and they succeeded in avoiding the graceful little gestures and lifeless pastorales of the later Zucarelli and Zais. We are now right in the heart of the new century, the eighteenth, and again painters felt the need to translate the truth of everyday life and to give expression to strength of feeling and a sincere state of mind.

The eye which now gathers the natural aspects of the world and its daily happenings, even the changes in the weather, cannot fail to see also the new man and his search for new ideals, which he finds in the day-to-day events around him. He feels himself too a part of these events, if not perhaps always their greatest interpreter. In the 'views' of Canaletto (Plate 22), we should not take into account only the artist's contemplation and absorption in the spectacle of the landscape; of great importance too is his rational perception of naked reality, unchanged by any imaginative comments of his own. This reality can become poetry by its concrete presence, rather than by its suggested appearance. As we appreciate more fully the value of the light which invades Canaletto's landscapes, so will it lose its theatrical character. In these landscapes there live human beings, no longer merely characters of the theatre. The portraits are so psychologically true, beneath the fringes and wigs of Rosalba Carriera, or in the family or street scenes of Pietro Longhi (Plate 24), that we can hear the vernacular and highly individual language of Goldoni's theatre, where the character was created in place of the mask.

The climate of renewed faith against which Venetian art of the new century unfolded influenced also another type of painting, both ecclesiastical and profane. Piazzetta (Plate 20) creates vertiginous figures in coloured smokes and zigzag spirals, who seem to possess the spirituality of celestial visions, while thrilling to the most cruel details of open wounds and mutilations of martyrs. A taste for the macabre mingles with mystic rapture in the artist's intense desire to achieve dramatic effect. From this almost melodramatic atmosphere come his lamps, his rosy wisps of smoke, his cascades of cold, whitish colours over the scaffolding of dark and inflamed shadows. The 'holy representation' becomes in Pittoni or Pellegrini a 'ballet,' where the characters move on tiptoe, pirouetting in contorted genuflexions in their silk clothes which flutter through the air reflecting haloes dissolving in a luminous dust. The graceful charms of Rococo find in these painters their most elegant and decadent expression. And among them too may sometimes be found Francesco Guardi (Plate 23) whose painting sparkles with an exquisite play of light and shade. He however always succeeded in saving his art from superfluous flourishes by an almost magical invention of reality. Guardi's fantastic images dissolve in the light, and his jerky brushstrokes break up the outlines with flashes of light.

Then Tiepolo (Plate 21) covered vast walls and ceilings with monumental figures under immense skies inhabited by ungirt women, mythological characters, angels and gnomes, in a sumptuous world of his imagination. This was the most sparkling period of Venetian light and colour and the culmination of an art conceived as a spectacle.

In the nineteenth century, the flame was again extinguished, at the time of the loss of national liberty. Yet we can agree with Rodolfo Pallucchini when he says that from Goya to Delacroix, from Manet to Cézanne, 'modern European painting speaks a language which is founded on the tradition created by five centuries of Venetian painting.'

Plate 1—PAOLO VENEZIANO: The Martyrdom of St Mark (*section of a polyptych*). A document dated 20th May 1343 authorised the deans of St Mark's Cathedral to spend 400 gold ducats for the purpose of providing a painted cover or box for the golden chalice which stood on the High Altar. This cover was known as a 'pala feriale,' that is, it was exhibited only on ferial days, and is now in the Cathedral museum. It is composed of two panels: in the upper part are figures of saints, and in the lower part are seven episodes from the *Life of St Mark*, among them the scene of the *Martyrdom*, which is reproduced here. At the foot of one section the date of the execution of this work is clearly marked: 22nd April 1345, and on the other side appears the signature of the painter and his collaborators —' Paolo Veneziano with Luca and Giovanni his sons painted this work.' This is not the first time that the name of Paolo Veneziano appears on an early Venetian painting. The *Dormitio Virginis* of Vicenza, painted before 1333, bears the signature ' Paulus de Viniciis,' which reappears in other paintings, and finally in the *Coronation of the Virgin* in the Frick Collection in New York. In this panel the name of the artist's son Giovanni again appears, with the date 1358. This is the last known work of Paolo. His death was referred to in a document of 1362. The ancon with polychrome reliefs in the Church of San Donato in Murano, which is dated 1310, has been attributed to Maestro Paolo as his earliest work, and we can therefore deduce that he must have been born not later than 1290.

Maestro Paolo is thus one of the first Venetian artists, and may be called the initiator of a most wonderful period in the history of art. The discovery of this early artist is one of the achievements of modern scholarship. Cavalcaselle classified four works as attributable to him in 1887, but one of these is not his work. But Evelyn Sandberg Vavalà, writing in 1930, was able to ascribe 29 works to him. And happily it can be said that in spite of the many hundreds of years which have elapsed, his works have passed down to us in large numbers.

If we compare Maestro Paolo with Giotto, Duccio or Simone Martini, his contemporaries, then he cannot be considered a master of their calibre, nor was he one of the reformers of Italian art. Yet his name is fundamental to a study of Venetian art, since in his work the pattern of that art is already clearly determined, and he may be placed beside Vitale da Bologna as one of the greatest originators of the flourishing art of panel painting.

He is usually considered a Byzantine artist, and he did in fact work under the strong influence of eastern art, which in Venice was continually strengthened both by the arrival of artists from Byzantium itself and through the intermediary of the neighbouring Ravenna. But the influence of this Byzantine art was attenuated by the painting of the mainland, which was quite different in style, either Romanesque or Gothic.

At that time Giotto was already working in Padua, and, at the same time, in Rimini artists were painting in a Giottesque manner, not far away from Venice. But it cannot be said that Paolo Veneziano was a follower of Giotto; especially as such a conception of art did not coincide with Venetian aspirations, and any similarities to Giotto in the painting of Paolo Veneziano appear in attenuated form by way of the artists of the Romagna. But it is obvious that Maestro Paolo was unable to ignore Giotto's different and stronger pictorial language. It was echoed particularly in his youthful works, such as the Murano ancon and the Dignano Polyptych dated 1321. But these works are not merely the repetitions of echoes; rather, they show lively and sincere affinities with Giotto's painting, which was re-lived so intensely by Paolo that it renewed his own conception, even when his painting became more decidedly Byzantine in character, and turned his mind towards Gothic forms.

It may cause surprise that Paolo should have turned towards Byzantine art at the time of his maturity, especially after his Vicenza panel of 1333, and it may be that such an academic form of Byzantism may have developed as the result of a journey to Constantinople. But he assumes the liturgical pomp, the decorative richness and the stylistic refinement of Byzantine art, while remaining at the same time a decidedly Romanesque artist with a strength and realism which belong to Gothic art.

His works have a bold narrative vigour, enhanced by lively gestures, with figures standing out in bold relief and a continual indication of spatial values, which although still empirical have yet reached a bold synthesis. We see this feeling for space in the *Martyrdom of St Mark*, which is placed in front of the monumental perspective of a ciborium, where the fearful scene is played out, and where there is a feeling for space which was unknown to Byzantine art.

Plate 2—ANTONIO PISANO called PISANELLO: Portrait of Lionello d'Este. It is barely half a century, after a long misunderstanding which clouded even the critical mind of Cavalcaselle, since we have become aware of the exceptional merit of this great master, Pisanello. He was the son of Puccio di Giovanni da Cereto, who a few days before he died made a will in his son's favour dated 22nd November 1395. His mother, Elisabetta di Niccolò of Verona remarried in the early fifteenth century and lived in Verona with her second husband, Bartolomeo da Pisa. Widowed a second time, she married again in 1414, and her third husband was the silk merchant, Filippo di Galvano di Ostiglia.

Pisanello's earliest work to reach us is the *Annunciation* in the Church of San Fermo in Verona (1426). This fresco was all by his own hand. The scene unfolds like a fable of a Gothic court; an angel with many-coloured wings appears to the châtelaine Virgin among marble fronds and leafy branches, before two tortoises and a small dog. We can see why it was that Pisanello painted in this refined and precious Gothic manner when we recall that between 1415 and 1420, and therefore at a very early age, Pisanello was summoned to Venice as a collaborator of Gentile da Fabriano, who was to decorate the Great Counsel Room of the Ducal Palace, now unfortunately destroyed. When his work in Venice was finished, Pisanello went to Florence, still together with Gentile, where he perhaps had a hand in that other jewelled fable, the *Adoration of the Magi*, now in the Uffizi. Unfortunately, his other youthful works have been lost: the frescoes which he painted in the Castle of Pavia in 1424, and those he painted in Mantua in the following year. In 1426 he was in Verona, where he was mentioned in a legal document as ' egregium pictorem.'

But Verona was not to benefit long from the genius of Pisanello: indeed in 1431 the artist was already in Ferrara, and soon after he was summoned to Rome to complete the frescoes in the Church of St John Lateran which had been left unfinished by the death of Gentile da Fabriano. These frescoes too were destroyed, when Borromini reconstructed the basilica.

Next we know that he wandered about from court to court in north Italy, from Ferrara to Milan, and to Mantua, as painter and medallist. In these courts there survived a Gothic pomp and culture which explains much of the ' international flavour ' of Pisanello's work. But between each voyage, in the years between 1433 and 1438, he found time to stop in Verona, to climb to the highest arch of the Pellegrini Chapel in the Church of Sant Anastasia and paint there the vast scene of St George departing for his combat with the Dragon and taking leave of the Princess. This painting seems to represent a chivalric tournament, a profane episode in which there is also a place for the cruel scene of the hanged, since become a holy legend. But now, within this Gothic refinement, there already appears not only the world of elegant fable, but an acute penetration into the reality of the natural world. And the almost painful sharpness of the drawing serves not so much to idealise the world, as to complete our knowledge of it and render its mysterious beauty. If Pisanello's artistic background was this mystical pagan environment of courtly Gothicism, his curiosity and senses were open to new developments at the threshold of the new humanism.

For his participation in a siege of Verona on behalf of the Duke of Mantua in 1439, Pisanello was exiled from Verona, and had to remain in Ferrara. The *Portrait of Lionello d'Este* was painted at this time: the profile as sharp as the relief of a medal, and of unequalled pictorial invention, even in Venice. But although he was not permitted to return to Verona, he was still to be found in the different courts at work on his medals; until in 1449 he was at the court of Alfonso of Aragona in Naples. What he did during the six years of his stay at the court of this splendid prince we have not yet been able to discover. There is every likelihood, though no actual proof, for the supposition, which has recently gained ground, that Pisanello worked together with a pupil on the fresco of the *Triumph of Death* in the Palazzo Sclafani in Palermo, where he may have left his portrait and that of his assistant. He died around 1455.

Plate 3—CARLO CRIVELLI: Virgin and Child. The dates of the birth and death of

Plate 2. ANTONIO PISANO called PISANELLO:
Portrait of Lionello d'Este. Panel, 28 x 19 cm. Bergamo, Accademia Carrara.

OPVS·CAROLI·CRIVELLI·VEN

Plate 3. CARLO CRIVELLI:
Virgin and Child. Panel 20 x 15 cm.
Ancona Art Gallery.

Plate 4. ANDREA MANTEGNA:
St George. Panel 66 x 32 cm.
Venice, Accademia Gallery.

the Venetian painter Carlo Crivelli are not known for certain, but it is possible to arrive at a close approximation. The first mention of Crivelli appears in a document of 7th March 1457, in which he is condemned for adultery and concubinage with Tarsia, the wife of a sailor, Francesco Cortese, to six months' imprisonment and 200 lire fine. In this document he is already described as a painter, a title given only to those who had completed their apprenticeship; and we can assume from the charge of adultery that he was already over twenty years old. Consequently, Crivelli may have been born between 1430 and 1435, and was therefore a contemporary of Giovanni Bellini and Mantegna.

In 1468 Crivelli was present in the Marches, in Massa Fermana, as we see from the signature and date of the polyptych in the parochial Church of San Silvestro, the earliest of his known works. From then onwards many documents and paintings confirm that he was present in the Marches region. In 1478 he bought a house at Ascoli Piceno in the district of San Biagio, near the Cathedral. But an act of September 1465 is evidence that Crivelli was then living in Zara and was a citizen, which indicates that he had been there for a long time.

It is therefore not difficult to conclude that, having paid his penalty, the young painter left the city and found refuge elsewhere. It is almost certain that he visited Padua, where there was a very lively interest in art, aroused by the works executed there by Donatello at that time and to the rising new star, Andrea Mantegna. In Padua Crivelli completed his artistic education, and while he did not lose his preference for the late Gothic art of the Vivarinis, he observed attentively the innovations of Mantegna in the Ovetari Chapel of the Church of the Eremitani. But from Mantegna's humanistic teaching he drew only what was particularly suited to his own temperament. So that, though he adopted the Renaissance formulae of plastic and perspective painting, he conveyed at the same time the pomp, elegance and chromatic decoration of Gothic painting with its shining abstract gold grounds.

In fact a long series of works show how long the painter remained faithful to Gothic art, even works on a very large scale, such as the *Madonna* of Corridonia, the Polyptych in Ascoli Cathedral dated 1473, the Polyptych in Montefiore dell' Aso, now broken up, the Polyptych of Camerino Cathedral, of which the famous *Virgin of the Candle* which dates from about 1490 forms part, the *Coronation of the Virgin*, a panel executed for the monks of Fabriano from 1493 and now in the Brera. The Gothic conception, it is true, was adapted to some of the principles of the art of the Renaissance, and above all to the artist's individual vision, which was one of superb formal elegance but also of such expressionistic excitement that it sometimes produced a feeling of cruelty. This impression of cruelty derives also from the mineral splendour of the colour, like that of precious stones, from the microscopic fidelity of detail and the incisive linear drawing. This insistence upon Gothic forms, which was still to be met in his work during the last years of his activity in the Marches, has caused Crivelli to be considered a retardatory painter, when this element in his work is compared with the Renaissance innovations in Florence and later in Padua and Venice, which were gathered up in a complex vision by Antonello and Giovanni Bellini. Some have also considered that in his last years Crivelli's painting declined into a more and more tired mannerism. But the recent exhibition in Venice dedicated to Crivelli has shown that while he may have rejected humanistic and Renaissance innovations because of his affinity with Gothic art, he was by no means a repetitive painter of mannerisms, because his work was always sustained by an authentic vision, which sought to renew from within the forms of Gothic painting.

The last note concerning this painter is dated 1494 and is to be found at Fabriano; he died before 7th August 1500, as in a document of that date his wife Iuranda is described as a widow.

The date of this *Virgin and Child* is not known for certain; but it is undoubtedly a work of the artist's maturity, with the characteristics of luxury, sumptuous decoration and minute detail which belong to that period of his work. The painting belonged to the Church of St Francis in Ancona, where it was brought to light in a sacristy cupboard in 1861.

Plate 5. ANDREA MANTEGNA:
The Death of the Virgin. Panel, 54 x 42 cm. Madrid, Prado.

Plate 4—ANDREA MANTEGNA: St George. On the altar-piece painted for the Church of Santa Sofia in Padua, according to Scardeone, there appeared the signature of Mantegna and the date, 1448, with the explicit declaration in Latin that he had painted it at the age of seventeen. This enables us to establish that Mantegna was born in 1431, and his place of birth was Isola di Carturo. From another document, however, it appears that at ten years of age he was in the studio of Francesco Squarcione, as his apprentice and adoptive son. Seven years later he had to ask for judiciary arbitration to enable him to be released from his guardian's control and regain his independence. If Squarcione taught him the first rudiments of painting, his artistic education was completed in Padua itself, where he was influenced by the paintings of Filippo Lippi for the Podestà Chapel, and the bronzes of Donatello executed for the Church of Il Santo. We see therefore that from his earliest formation, which was evidently based on the example of Vivarini, as we see from the *Polyptych of St Luke* which he painted for the Church of Santa Giustina in 1453-4 and is now in the Brera, Mantegna was ahead of his time in his deep attachment to the new forms and visions of Renaissance art. The Ovetari Chapel in the Church of the Eremitani in Padua bore witness to this transformation. The painting of this chapel was begun in 1448 and for various reasons the work dragged on until 1455. After the death of Pizzolo and Giovanni d'Alemagna, and Antonio Vivarini's withdrawal from the work, Mantegna found himself without colleagues, left to sustain alone the responsibility for the great undertaking of completing the frescoes which they had contracted to paint. This chapel was tragically destroyed by bombs which fell on 11th March 1944, and the paintings were broken up. A large collection of photographs, taken before the disaster, show the young Mantegna to have been one of the greatest painters of the new Renaissance style. It may even be said that no one else accepted and developed to the same extent the Renaissance ideas of perspective, of plasticity or of recourse to ancient monuments: which in fact crowd his paintings with columns, arches, capitals, architraves, and sculptural fragments, in a lucid archaeological reconstruction.

The fame brought to Mantegna by these Paduan frescoes and the altar screen for the Church of San Zeno in Verona caused him to be summoned to Mantua to the court of Marquis Ludovico Gonzaga. The Marquis treated him as his close confidant, as well as official painter of his household. Many works were painted by Mantegna at the Gonzaga court, where he remained for about half a century. The most important of these, and indeed one of the masterpieces of the Italian Renaissance, is the so-called 'Nuptial Room'; the Marquis appears together with his wife and children, with ambassadors and court personages, in an ideal assembly, within the portals of the palace and against a broad landscape. In this work, with its combination of humanism and a splendid power of representation, Mantegna shows too his interest in the great paintings of Piero della Francesca in Arezzo.

After the death of the Marquis Ludovico, Mantegna continued to work for his successors, among whom was Isabella d'Este, a most cultured and refined woman. She asked Mantegna for some 'allegories' to decorate a small study, and Mantegna painted *Parnassus*, and *Minerva Driving Away the Vices*. By the side of these paintings, Isabella had other 'allegories' painted by Perugino and Costa. These were among the last works of Mantegna, and before he began them he painted, between 1485 and 1492, the famous cartoons depicting scenes of the *Triumph of Caesar*. These cartoons were sold by the Gonzagas in 1629 and are now to be seen in Hampton Court, as part of the Queen's collection. From a letter sent by his son Francesco to the Marquis in Perugia on 15th September 1506, we learn that the great artist expired two days earlier at seven in the evening. Mantegna was buried in the mortuary chapel of the Church of Sant' Andrea in Mantua which he had prepared for himself and his family.

The painting of *St George* reveals the classical conception of Mantegna's painting. The young saint seems to recall an ancient divinity or a Roman hero. The relief and the masterly linear perspective create a sculptural effect. The attitude is calm and serene, as is fitting for a classical hero. This painting was no doubt executed during the first years of Mantegna's life at the court of Mantua.

Plate 5—ANDREA MANTEGNA: The Death of the Virgin. Mantegna had recently finished the paintings for the Ovetari Chapel in the Church of the Eremitani in Padua, and had barely started the great altar-piece of St Zeno for the Veronese church of that name, when he received the first invitation from the Marquis Ludovico Gonzaga to move to the court of Mantua. On 5th January 1457 he sent his acceptance, but asked first to be allowed to finish the painting he had just started. Three years were spent on that work, and in the meantime Gonzaga wrote impatiently to ask him to hurry and asked friends and acquaintances to persuade the artist to place himself at his service. We learn from these letters that Mantegna was occupied in finishing the chapel of the palace (June 1459); while in a letter of 26th April 1464, Mantegna, who was then in Goito, complained that the frames for the paintings he wished to place in the chapel would not be ready by the end of the month. This means that at that date the paintings were already completed.

In another document of later date, a decree of 1492 by the Marquis Francesco Gonzaga, the 'Nuptial Room, the nine cartoons of the *Triumph of Caesar*, and the paintings in the chapel in Mantua, are cited among the greatest paintings undertaken by Mantegna for the Gonzagas. But what these paintings in the chapel were, or how these panels were disposed, is not known exactly. However, various conjectures have been made, and it is believed that they are the so-called *Triptych of the Uffizi*, which already in 1587 belonged to Antonio Medici before it passed in 1632 to the Grand Dukes of Tuscany. This *Triptych* is composed of three panels representing, in the centre, the *Adoration of the Magi*, and at the sides, the *Circumcision* and the *Ascension*.

But it is obvious that as this was described as one of the greatest works undertaken by the artist, the three small panels must have been only a part of the decoration of the Castle Chapel, now no longer in existence. It is not known what the other paintings may have been.

However in 1926 Longhi mentioned the panel depicting the *Death of the Virgin* in the Prado as being from the same work as the panels composing the Florentine Triptych; and in 1934 Longhi also brilliantly showed that the panel had been cut and that the missing part, which represented *Christ Receiving the Soul of the Virgin in Heaven*, according to Byzantine iconography, is the fragment in the Barbicinti Collection, now the Baldi Collection, in Ferrara.

This panel of the *Death of the Virgin* was sold in 1627 to Charles I of England, and from his collection it later passed to Spain. According to Fiocco, the composition derives from the mosaic in the Mascoli Chapel in St Mark's, Venice; while Longhi believed the connection to be the reverse—the mosaic being executed not by Mantegna but by one of his followers.

Certainly the work is of rare beauty and painted at the time of the artist's maturity. From the inside of the room, where the Apostles are gathered around the bed of the dead Virgin, to the opening which leads the eye to the luminous and vast landscape in the background, there is a progression in perspective of rare skill and simplicity of design. The figures of the apostles, though minute, recall the marble monumentality of the gigantic figures of the saints which appear in the painting of St Zeno. But the colour in this small panel is much livelier. This is perhaps because of the luminosity of the landscape, with its waters which reflect the blue of the sky, and its two large surfaces sparkling with diffused light. As long as this painting was believed to be by Carpaccio, it was thought that this landscape represented a part of the Lagoon. But after Longhi correctly ascribed it to Mantegna, the landscape has been variously associated with diverse localities of the Mantuan lake around the Castello. We may well think this fragment of Mantegna to be one of the greatest landscape paintings of all time.

Plate 6—GIOVANNI BELLINI: Pietà (*detail*). As the eldest son of Jacopo Bellini, Gentile, was born in 1429, the other son Giovanni must have been born not before 1430. This date coincides with the earliest works we know of this painter: the landscape *Crucifixion* in the Correr Museum, *St Ursula among*

her Companions in the Gallery of Venice and the *Virgin and Child* in the Museum of Pavia. These works were all painted between 1450 and 1460, at the time when the artistic education of the young painter was based on the examples of his father, and above all on the Muranese painter Antonio Vivarini.

But with the four triptychs executed after 1462 for the Carità Church, Giovanni Bellini came very much under the influence of Mantegna, who was known in Padua. Therefore the influence of the Florentine Renaissance reached the Venetian artist through Filippo Lippi and Donatello by way of the Paduan Mantegna. This situation was prolonged for more than ten years, until the *Coronation of the Virgin*, painted about the year 1473 for Pesaro. The great work of this Mantegnesque period, besides the *Polyptych of San Vincenzo Ferrer*, is the *Pietà* in the Brera which was painted about 1470. Mantegna had studied in antiquity for models to inspire the new painting; and he had in fact created the marmoreal giants and heroes of the archaeological Ovetari frescoes, the altar-pieces of St Zeno and St George in Venice. The example of Mantegna dominates the whole of Venetian painting; and hence it was soon to dominate the painting of Giovanni Bellini. But Bellini was an authentically creative artist, and he introduced into the subtle and dogmatic classicism of Mantegna a new warmth of feeling which is lacking in his great colleague; and this new feeling is expressed in the painting of Bellini through a more noticeable effect of light which softens the somewhat stony harshness of Mantegna. This is the most vital distinction between the two painters and will take on more and more significance. It can best be seen in this *Pietà* in the Brera, here reproduced. The three figures, placed against a gentle sky which occupies almost the entire space, are embracing, and their hands seek each other to form knots of anxious grief. The great sculptural composition loses some of its marmoreal quality by a play of soft lights which helps to define the relief, filling the cavities with warm shadows. The sorrow of these characters will be one of the main sources of Giovanni Bellini's inspiration.

The *Coronation* in Pesaro, painted about 1473, reveals the artist's firm allegiance to Piero della Francesca's monumental conceptions composed in broad and harmonious masses. With this work a new attitude to perspective was born, no longer linear as Mantegna's had been, but chromatic, just as the most obvious innovation of Piero had indicated. Antonello too, who arrived in Venice about 1475, was to be influenced by this conception. And it was this very feeling for space and luminous colour, for perspective harmony and warmth of feeling which was to determine the course of Venetian painting. The great fundamental works of Giovanni Bellini are: the *Transfiguration* in Naples, painted about 1485, and *Altar-piece of St Job* of about 1488, the *Baptism of Christ* for the Church of Santa Corona in Vicenza, dated 1502. The composition is now placed in the heart of a sunny landscape, impregnated with a tenderness not previously found in Italian painting. It is by this new and deeper expression of light and colour that Giovanni Bellini was able to open the way first to Giorgione and then to Titian. He made use of examples introduced by Piero and Antonello, but they evolved in a way which was typically his own, in which his desire to give prominence to warmth of feeling removed the divine characters from the field of ideal abstraction and transformed them into human figures. This is also the recognisable sign of his last works, such as the Altar-pieces for San Zaccaria of 1505, and the Altar-pieces for St John Chrysostom of 1513. We know from a note in the diary of Marin Sanudo that the painter died, an old man, November 1516.

Plate 7—GIOVANNI BELLINI: St George Conquers the Dragon. Among the different and always characteristic evolutions of Giovanni Bellini's art, as it came into contact with great paintings of his time to develop a more and more complex and profound harmony of its own, we have recalled the influence of Piero della Francesca. Piero's work raised new problems for artists who seemed already to have achieved complete maturity: Mantegna or Antonello for example. Piero's influence on Venetian art was to be developed by way of Giovanni Bellini. His use of light, or rather, his feeling for a perspective of light and colour, enabled Bellini to achieve

Plate 6. GIOVANNI BELLINI:
Pietà (detail). Panel 86 x 107 cm. Milan, Brera Art Gallery.

Plate 7. GIOVANNI BELLINI:
St George Conquers the Dragon (section of predella).
Panel, 43 x 36 cm. Pesaro, Civic Museum.

Plate 8. ANTONELLO DA MESSINA:
Portrait. Panel, 34 x 25 cm. London, National Gallery.

a greater depth of expression.

His encounter with the painting of Piero must have been a true revelation. Giovanni Bellini had been called to execute the great altar-piece for the Church of St Francis in Pesaro; and we may recognise some local landscapes in his paintings of this period: a little after 1470, for example, the Rock of Gradara in this screen, and in other paintings some monuments from Ravenna or Rimini. It can therefore be deduced that the work was painted in Pesaro, for which reason Bellini travelled to the Marches. It was during this journey that the young Venetian saw the original paintings of Piero, in Ferrara, Rimini, Pesaro and Urbino. These paintings made a deep impression on Bellini. Roberto Longhi has spoken with acute insight of the 'capital direction taken by the art of Giovanni Bellini,' and Pallucchini too confirms that it was from this moment that Bellini threw off Mantegna's influence and turned to the new perspective synthesis of form and colour, created by Piero della Francesca.

This great altar-piece of the *Coronation of the Virgin* was mentioned again as 'precious and renowned' by a scholar of Pesaro in 1806, and is still to be seen in the Church of St Francis. The *Pietà*, formerly above it, was removed in 1797, but was recovered by Canova and is now in the Vatican Museum, where for many years it was ascribed to Mantegna.

The work consists of a large painting representing the Coronation of the Virgin by Christ. Around the great white marble throne with polychrome decorations there appear four figures of saints: Paul, Peter, Jerome and Francis. The back of the throne rises against a blue sky, and an amazing innovation is the large square window in the marble back of the throne which enables us to glimpse the Pesaro landscape in the background, with the hills, the clumps of trees and the battlements of the castle. Eight pilasters with eight figures of saints surround the central picture, while the predella is composed of seven sections representing different scenes from the lives of the saints. The left division of this predella represents St George on horseback slaying the dragon. The horse recalls the drawing made some years earlier by his father Jacopo, in his sketchbook which is now in London, in the British Museum.

But the most surprising innovation of this painting is the new feeling for space in the freedom of movement, as if the Gothic rigidity which had stiffened figures so that they appeared like statues against a gold ground or the pale image of a conventional lanscape had become unloosed. The dimensions of each section are rather small, yet in spite of that, the landscape appears grandiose owing to the airy circulation of the light passing through the gradated thicknesses of the atmosphere. And seen against the rock-like linear perspective of Mantegna, colour here enhances the effect of distance, with a tender play of shades and reflections. We can easily see how from a painting like this one in Pesaro there could emerge the two great Venetian painters, Giorgione and Titian. It is thanks to Giovanni Bellini that a new connection between colour and light entered Venetian painting; and the initial work of this capital transformation is this Pesaro altar-piece.

Plate 8—ANTONELLO DA MESSINA: Portrait. The painting here reproduced is believed to be a self-portrait. This belief is founded on the existence of an inscription which was formerly at the foot of the picture, was subsequently copied on to the back, but has now disappeared. The painting belonged to a Genoese family, the Molfini, whose connections with Sicily during the fifteenth century can be traced in several legal documents. The probable date of the painting is 1470. This date has been fixed for reasons of style, even though the man portrayed appears to be younger than Antonello was at that time.

According to Vasari, Antonello died at the age of 49. On 25th February 1479, Antonello's son, Jacobello, who was himself a painter, renewed the contract which his father had made a little earlier to produce a standard for a donor of Randazzo; and on this occasion, Jacobello confirmed that his father 'had emigrated towards another light.' About ten days earlier, on 14th February, Antonello dictated his will, in which his father, Giovanni d'Antonio, a marble worker, and his mother, Margherita, were mentioned as being alive. From calculations made on the basis of Vasari's

Plate 9. ANTONELLO DA MESSINA:
Annunciation. 45 x 34.5 cm. Palermo, Museo Nazionale.

information, Antonello must have been born around 1430.

This date coincides, too, both with the influences around him and with the early documents which mention his works. In 1456 he had a pupil, the Calabrian Paolo du Ciacio; this means that he already had his own workshop and could act as a master. On 5th March 1457, he undertook to paint a standard in the Sicilian manner, that is of carved wood with a central panel painted on both sides, for the Confraternity of San Michele dei Gerbini in Reggio di Calabria; in that contract, another standard was mentioned as an example, the standard made for the Confraternity of St Michael in Messina. These are the two first paintings of Antonello which have been mentioned, and unfortunately they have not come down to us. A Neapolitan scholar, Summonte, in a letter of 1524, stated that the young artist from Messina was a pupil of Colantonio, a painter working in Naples. So that, between the year of his birth, as indicated by Vasari, and the document of Messina concerning his pupil, it can be argued that Antonello was in Naples with Colantonio, and travelling about from place to place, between 1445 and 1455. In these early years, a number of works have been definitely ascribed to him, among them the dramatic *Crucifixion* in Sibiu in Roumania, with a deep landscape in which can be distinguished the port of his city and the distant islands; the two small panels in the museum of Reggio di Calabria representing the *Three Angels* and *St Jerome in Penitence*; also *St Jerome in his Study*, now in the National Gallery in London, which contains an individual conception of perspective and an interest in fine detail, in which some scholars have seen a Flemish influence, while it might perhaps be due to the influence of Provençal art, which reached Antonello by way of Colantonio and the Master of the Annunciation of Aix.

With these paintings, we have come close to the *Salvator Mundi* in London, his first dated work, marked 1465. In this painting, Antonello, together with certain details painted in the Flemish manner, showed his allegiance to the perspective teaching of Piero della Francesca, not only in the monumental frontality of the bust of Christ, but especially in the hands, so carefully disposed, one on the short baluster and the other suspended in mid-air. It is indeed not unlikely that Antonello had at some time studied the frescoes of Piero in the Vatican. For example, we know with certainty that on 15th January 1460 his father hired a brigantine to go to Amantea, on the Calabrian coast, to meet his son and family on their return from a voyage. We do not know the details of this voyage, and many suppositions have been made: some believe that Antonello was returning from Flanders, but he might equally have been on his way home from much nearer, perhaps from Rome.

From that time onwards, his paintings follow each other for fifteen years with a calm rhythm and progressive pictorial skill. Among others, there is the ironical *Portrait* in Cefalù, the *Portrait* in London, the Virgin Annunciate with folded arms in Munich, the *Polyptych of St Gregory* (1473) in Messina, and the *Ecce Homo* in Piacenza, painted in the same year. Then in 1475 he painted the *Crucifixion*, now in Antwerp, which led to the great works testifying to his presence in Venice, works of such importance that they renewed the course of Venetian painting: the *Pietà* in the Correr Museum, the *San Cassiano Altar-piece* (1476), the fragments of which are in Vienna, and the Dresden *St Sebastian* with its admirably foreshortened Venetian landscape. In September 1476, he was again in Messina, and little more than two years later he dictated the will which has been referred to.

Plate 9—ANTONELLO DA MESSINA: Annunciation. For a long time this Virgin of the Annunciation, an adolescent black-eyed Sicilian, in Arab dress, was believed to be not the work of Antonello but a variant of the copy existing in the Accademia Gallery in Venice. The painting was first mentioned as being in the house of the Colluzio family in Palermo, and is now universally counted among the masterpieces of Antonello da Messina. This superb composition, with the brilliantly foreshortened reading desk with open book placed to one side, so as to make the timorous gesture of the hand appear free; the limpid light shining on the face and creating reflections of shadow right into the cavity formed by the closed cloak in a triangle on the neck; and the ivory toned colour which invests the pure forms with a gentle velvet warmth, all point to this being a work of the artist's maturity, painted when he had already completed many masterpieces, including his work in Venice, and had achieved a fusion between the rigour of Renaissance composition and subtle colour effects. Since Antonello was in Venice from 1475, this *Annunciation*, unlike the earlier *Annunciation* in Munich, must belong to the last years of the painter's life, about 1477-8.

Naturally, this painting too has been said to be influenced by Flemish painting. It is difficult to deny this influence, and mention has been made in this connection of the great Bruges artist Jan van Eyck, who, however, died in 1441 when Antonello was only eleven years of age. Vasari also wrote that Antonello went to Flanders, and that from there he may have imported the method of painting in oils instead of in tempera, which was the method still employed in Italy. It is in connection with that journey that mention has been made of the brigantine hired by Antonello's father on 15th January 1460, to go to Amantea in Calabria, where he met Antonello, accompanied by his wife, children, brothers, father-in law and other families coming from no one knows where. Some critics have held that Antonello may have met, in the Sforza court in Milan, Pietro Burgensis, identified with Petrus Christus from Bruges, who was a pupil of van Eyck. However, the documentary dates belie this meeting.

Besides, even if he did not go to Flanders, he may have absorbed Flemish culture by other means, for example, during his apprenticeship in Naples with Colantonio, which occurred within the ten years 1445-55. Naples at that time, first under Robert of Anjou and then Alfonso of Aragon, was a generous meeting-place for many European cultures, including the painting of Flanders, Spain and Provence, as well as the regions of Italy. Colantonio was not immune to these foreign influences; and in consequence, Antonello too was affected by them. Beside the Flemish painting of Jan van Eyck and Rogier van der Weyden, Antonello was probably surrounded by a fruitful circulation of ideas, among which we can see traces in his youthful works of the Spaniards, Jacomart and Huguet, and the French painters, the Master of the Annunciation of Aix and Fouquet.

But a deeper and more lasting influence on Antonello was the painting of Piero della Francesca. Antonello probably met Piero in Rome when he was quite young, as by 1475 when he was in Venice, he had absorbed Piero's influence for a long time. At an early age, according to Vasari, Antonello spent a considerable time in Rome where he sketched, and the fruit of his meeting with Piero was a Flemish psychological predilection for minute detail which he absorbed into the perspective by his monumental sense of form coinciding with human figure. From here there came Antonello's feeling for spatial relationships and for geometrical shapes, and his psychological penetration reveals the intimate thoughts of his characters, while not lessening the architectonic quality of the figures: from the irony of the Cefalù *Portrait* to the liveliness of the *Portrait* in London, and finally the hard arrogance of the Louvre *Condottiero*.

His work in Venice brought to the Sicilian artist a richer colouring; until in the *San Cassiano Altar-piece* Antonello created a new pictorial organism, a correspondence between the mutually dependent architecture and colour. We may therefore conclude that while Antonello learned something from Venetian painting, he in his turn exercised an influence on that painting, as witness the works of Giovanni Bellini and Carpaccio.

Plate 10—VITTORE CARPACCIO: Meeting of St Ursula with Pope Ciriaco (*detail*). The first mention of Carpaccio, a Venetian painter, appears in a will drawn up by an uncle, who was a friar, on 21st September 1472, where he nominated as heirs some of his relatives, including his nephew Vittore. But we have no indication from this will of the probable date of the painter's birth; nor can this be deduced from the references made to him either by his widow Laura, who certified that her husband was still alive on 28th October 1525, or by his son Pietro, who on 26th June 1526 indicated that he was then dead. Judging from the style of his paintings, which were few in the early part of his

VICTORIS · CAR
PATIO · VENETI
OPVS ·

Plate 11. GIORGIONE DA CASTELFRANCO:
The Tempest. Canvas, 78 x 72 cm. Venice, Accademia Gallery.

Plate 10. VITTORE CARPACCIO:
Meeting of St Ursula with Pope Ciriaco (detail).
Canvas, 281 x 307 cm. Venice, Accademia Gallery.

life and numerous as from 1490, when he signed the first cartoons of the cycle of the legends of the *Life of St Ursula*, to which this painting belongs, we are now inclined to believe that Carpaccio was born around 1465.

But he must have been considered an excellent painter at a very early age, for the School of St Ursula began to set aside money for these paintings as early as 1488, and entrusted such a vast and important task to him, although he was then only about 25 years old. The series is composed of nine cartoons: the cartoon representing the *Arrival at Cologne*, the earliest in date, is dated ' September 1490,' and is the first signed and dated painting of Carpaccio to have reached us. Other dates appear on the other cartoons, so that we know that in 1496 the whole work was completed. It was indeed a great success, both for the splendid painting and for the narrative talent of Carpaccio, who appeared as the recorder of the daily events of his time as well as the inventor of a fabulous profane world. Carpaccio was in fact the first painter who dared to transfer the reality of daily events in the lives of the common people of his city to a place among the episodes of holy legend. In his painting of the *Miracle of the Holy Cross*, executed for the School of St John the Evangelist, the miracle of the curing of the man possessed by demons is placed to one side, almost relegated to the margin, while the whole painting is dedicated to the glorious motion of the gondolas along the Grand Canal, the houses and marble buildings, and the procession of the people, among whom are gondoliers and people of the neighbourhood in fantastically coloured clothes.

The success of the St Ursula paintings made it possible for Carpaccio to execute other series of paintings, and in fact the Venetians vied with each other in entrusting to him tasks of this kind. After his collaboration on the paintings in the School of St John the Evangelist, he painted a whole cycle, again of nine cartoons, for the School of San Giovanni degli Schiavoni, between 1502 and 1510; then another series for the Scuola degli Albanesi, and finally a series painted for the Scuola di Santo Stefano, now in the Brera, in which, having absorbed the teaching of Gentile Bellini and ready for the architectonic conception of Antonello, Carpaccio is then influenced by the last paintings of Giovanni Bellini, with their colour softened by light. We see therefore that while Carpaccio was occupied in creating the fable of his ' pictorial tales,' he did not lose contact with the development of Venetian art.

The minute details, which fill the paintings of the various cycles, as if each object were looked at through a magnifying glass, denote an affinity with Flemish art: but the artist also discovered and expressed the natural beauty of the world as if it were an invention of his own inspiration. And yet, as Antonello has indicated, the monumentality of his visions is never diminished. The artist's world of fantasy has a feeling of cosmic grandeur which gives importance to even the smallest and most neglected detail. For that reason, Carpaccio is not to be belittled as a fabulist of genius, enchanted by his own inventions. He should rather be considered an investigator into natural form, whose ' tales ' as they unfold demonstrate the beauty implicit in the physical appearance of the universe; and for that reason too he is in line with the greatest artists of the Italian Renaissance.

Plate 11—GIORGIONE DA CASTELFRANCO: The Tempest. No official document indicates, even indirectly, the dates of the birth and death of Giorgione da Castelfranco, who was one of the greatest of Venetian painters and a universally esteemed genius. From a letter of 25th October 1510 of Isabella d'Este, we learn of the death of Giorgione (and the answer of her agent in Venice, Taddeo Albano, confirms that his death was due to the plague). For the date of his birth we can only rely on Vasari. In the first edition of his *Lives* in 1550, he states: ' in Castelfranco above Trevisano was born in the year 1477, Giorgio, for the features of his person and the greatness of his soul later called Giorgione '; and Vasari again adds: ' he continually delighted in matters of love, and he liked the sound of the lute wonderfully.'

The first document which definitely refers to Giorgione is dated 14th August 1507. This was an order by the Council of Ten to pay Giorgione twenty ducats for a painting which was to be placed in the Audience Room, now no longer in existence. Also accepted as being by Giorgione are the frescoes in the Fondaco dei Tedeschi, on the Grand Canal, which were completed on 8th November 1508. In his report of 12th December of that year, Giorgione declared himself satisfied to receive 130 ducats; but from these frescoes there have come down to us only the engravings made by Zanetti, and some fragments of figures, now reduced to meagre phantoms of colour. Owing to the uncertain documentary evidence, the fame which soon surrounded Giorgione in his lifetime inspired early writers to create a literary myth around him. This myth is fascinating, but too rich in invention; and with the myth around the person of the artist, many works too began to be ascribed to him which are still the source of lively discussion among scholars. For this reason, the basis of every inventory of Giorgione's works still remains the notes begun as far back as 1525 by Marcantonio Michiel.

Vasari mentions that Giorgione was apprenticed to Giovanni Bellini, and this is not disputed, although it has not been proved. Bellini was, of course, the greatest artist of those years, and his example must in any case have influenced the young Giorgione, who was himself inclined to sentiment. He may also have felt an interest in the painting of Carpaccio, with its narrative, lucid form, rich in lively comments on the everyday world. Nor can we overlook Leonardo's visit to Venice in 1500, and the probable meeting which took place between the two artists. An examination of the early works of Giorgione—the two paintings in the Uffizi, the *Boy with the Arrow* in Vienna, and the *Shepherd with Flute* in Hampton Court—supports these suppositions. In the same way, the *Castelfranco Altar-piece,* where the Virgin is enthroned above a summer landscape of hills and castles, with the two saints at the foot of the throne, reveals certain affinities with the art of Emilia and Umbria. From these diverse influences, then, Giorgione developed a new kind of painting. In the words of Vasari, 'in the colouring with oil and with fresco he made some lively works and other things soft and smooth, and blended in the dark colours.'

His painting was new too for its poetical feeling. The classical dream of fifteenth century artists, from Mantegna to Giovanni Bellini, was expressed in formal themes and examples repeated from ancient art. It was realised by Giorgione through a less archaeological treatment, but through his wonder and love for the beauties of nature, his deep landscapes and calm and ample variations of light. The world of humanistic idealism has become a world of dreams, aroused by a lyrical emotion which takes possession of the artist's soul. And the religiosity of Giovanni Bellini, which invests his divine personages with human sentiments, now envelopes the created world in a mysterious vision. Giorgione created a subtle world of reality interwoven with his vivid imagination; we see this in such superb paintings as the *Three Philosophers* in Vienna, the so-called *Twilight*, formerly in Venice, in the Donà delle Rose collection, and, most famous of all, the *Tempest*, in the Accademia Gallery.

Some have looked for an allegorical meaning in this painting. But probably it was meant to express no more than a sweet enchantment of the senses and imagination, in a moment of extreme poetical tension. Every detail of the scene, the landscape of houses and towers against a sky traversed by stormy lightning flashes, the uprooted columns, and the figures placed among the branches on the bank of a river which has been flowing since time immemorial, is tense with emotion, and its subtle harmony has created a whole world of lyrical feeling.

Plate 12—TIZIANO VECELLIO: The Magdalen. No one now accepts the year 1477 as the date of birth at Pieve di Cadore of Tiziano Vecellio. It is true that Titian himself has given weight to this as the date of his birth, but other information given by him or by persons closely following him has made it possible to assign a date between 1485 and 1490 as being more probable, in view too of the first references to his paintings. These include, for example, the work done in collaboration with Giorgione in 1508-09 on the frescoes in the Fondaco dei Tedeschi; and the earliest document referring to him is dated 2nd December 1511, in which Titian is granted four gold ducats by the School of the Saint

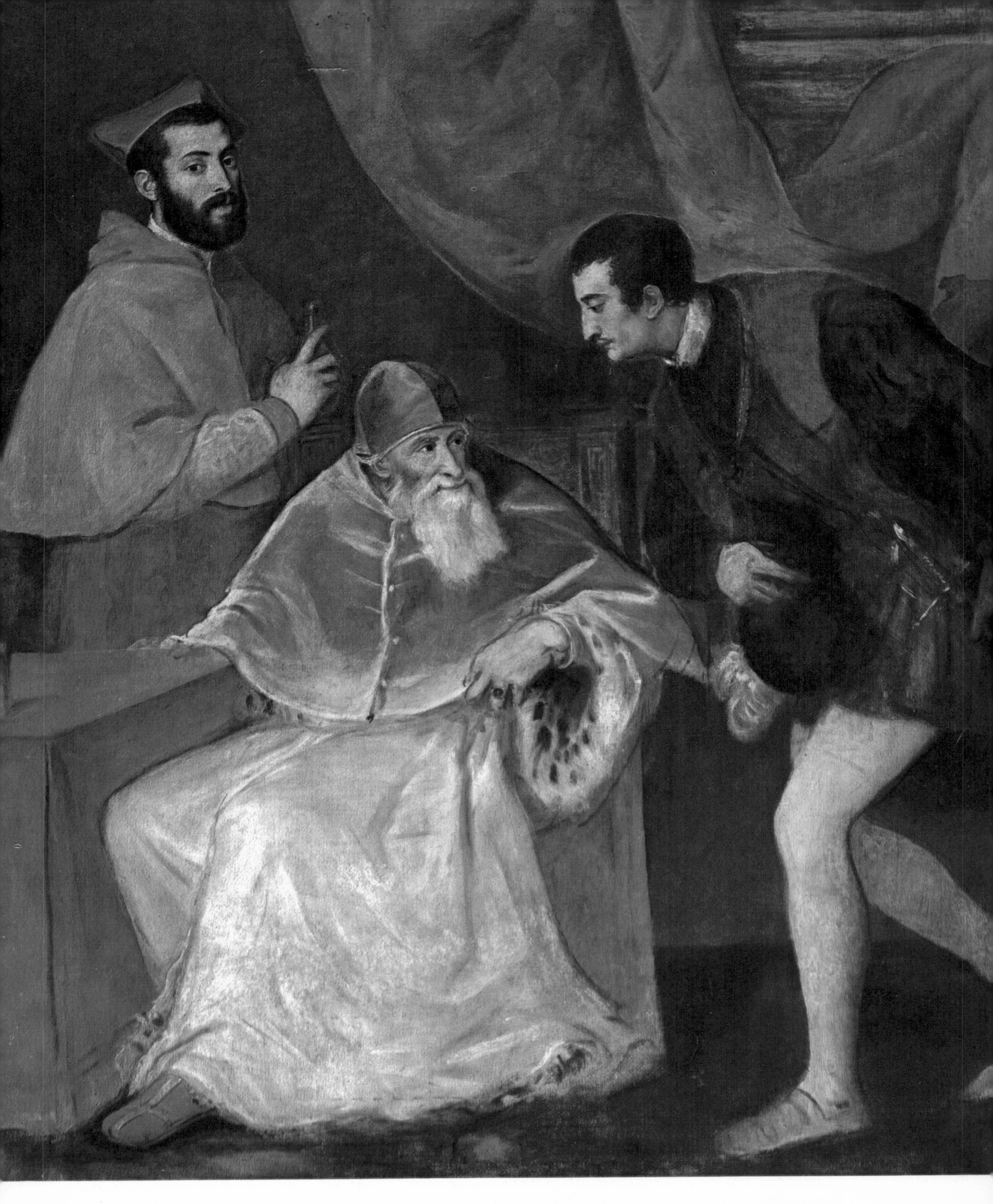

Plate 13. TIZIANO VECELLIO:
Pope Paul III Farnese with his Nephews.
Canvas, 201 x 174 cm. Naples, Capodimonte Museum.

Plate 12. TIZIANO VECELLIO:
The Magdalen. Panel, 85 x 68 cm. Florence, Pitti Palace.

in Padua in payment of the three frescoes of the *Miracles of the Saint*, which are still to be found there. If we accepted the year 1477 as his date of birth, we would have had a silence of more than 30 years, which would be too long even for a tardy painter.

The youthful work of Titian is now seen to be interwoven with that of the now old Giovanni Bellini, and especially, with that of Giorgione. Many of Giorgione's paintings were in fact finished or worked on to a greater or lesser extent by Titian: the *Concert* in the Louvre, the *Venus* in Dresden, the *Concert* in the Pitti Palace. So we can see in what surroundings the artist was formed and developed. Compared with Giorgione, Titian had a more concrete vision of reality, and to his dreamy and ideal atmosphere Titian opposes a more direct sense of reality, with figures of greater psychological insight and of more monumental presence. That is why even the colour, as well as the composition itself, is adapted to this concrete representation. This can be seen also in the painting known as *Sacred and Profane Love*. Although this is an allegorical work, rich in symbols or reminiscences of ancient art, Titian translates it into contemporary terms. And this is not only because of the warm carnality of the women, but also the landscape against which the action takes place, in a tranquil hour of the afternoon, with horses running alongside the lake and flocks resting under the trees.

Many works of this decade overflow with life in this way. It is expressed in the ample gestures and virile presence of the characters and the sonorous timbre of the colour. In the *Assumption of the Virgin*, begun on the altar of the Frari Church on 20th March 1518, the circle of figures and light seems to inflame the atmosphere. With this painting, which was to become the prototype of Venetian sixteenth-century altar-pieces, Titian appeared as the new master. The *Pesaro Altar-piece* after the family of the donor, was installed, also in the Frari Church, in 1526, although it was begun in 1519. This work was another bold step forward in Titian's conquest of space and light. In it, moreover, the figures of the Virgin and the Saints are as corporeal and imminent as the figures who compose the Pesaro family. The man holds himself and his humanity in such high consideration that he can stand freely by the side of the celestial figures, without for that reason reducing the religious representation to profanity.

Such a conception was most pleasing to the princely courts. They were then living through the period of their greatest splendour. As early as 1516, Titian had come into contact with Alfonso I d'Este, to whom he sent paintings and portraits for the court of Ferrara; in 1523 he opened relations with Frederick II, Marquis of Mantua, to whom he was to send two years later the dramatic *Deposition*, which in 1627 was sold to Charles I of England, and was later acquired by Louis XIV for the Louvre. In 1533, Charles V, Emperor of Spain, named him palatine count. From then on, there was no European court which did not wish to possess a painting or portrait by Titian. Even Pope Paul III Farnese wanted him to go to the Vatican to paint the famous series of portraits which are now in the National Gallery of Naples.

In 1531 he painted, for the Marquis of Mantua, the *Magdalen* here reproduced. The Marquis wanted to give the painting to Davalos del Vasto, the favourite of Charles V; but the painting came into the possession of the Duke of Urbino, and just a century later, under the inheritance of Vittoria Della Rovere, reached Florence. The model seems to be taken from an ancient Venus, and it unites Christian penitence with pagan sensuality in a superb pictorial synthesis.

Plate 13—TIZIANO VECELLIO: Pope Paul III Farnese With his Nephews. About the year 1540 the fame of Michelangelo began to reach Venice for his work in the Vatican and the Sixtine Chapel. Even Titian began to be affected by this influence. A period of ' mannerism ' began, and lasted a few years. In the paintings executed in the course of those five years, the amplitude of Titian's luminous colour became diminished, and he turned to more sculptural forms, giving the bodies greater plastic relief as had been done by Michelangelo. Michelangelo however was not at all aware of the chromatic problems which constituted the great innovation of Titian's painting.

This new conception, so different from his search after atmospheric colour impregnated with light, appears in the three canvases painted by Titian for the sacristy ceiling in the Salute Church in Venice, with superb foreshortening of the statuesque figures, and in the great altar-piece painting of the *Crowning with Thorns*, executed about 1542 for the Church of Le Grazie in Milan. This new conception does not represent a lessening of Titian's creative faculty, but only a deviation towards problems which did not coincide at all either with the prevailingly chromatic tradition of Venetian art, or with his own conception of painting steeped in atmospheric luminosity.

On the occasion of the visit of Pope Paul III to Ferrara, Titian went there to paint the full length portrait. Two years later, the Pope again invited Titian to Rome, where he arrived in October 1545 with the suite of the Duke of Urbino. Welcomed like a prince, Titian was invited to stay in the Vatican Belvedere (where Michelangelo and Vasari went to visit him). During his stay in Rome, Titian painted two large works: the *Danae*, and the portrait of the Pope with his nephews, Cardinal Alessandro Farnese and Ottavio, who was to become the son-in-law of Charles V. And we may say that, right in the enemy territory of his great rival, Titian found faith in his own principles and inventions. Besides its sharp psychological penetration, this triple portrait excels in its bold invention in colour, for the superb combination of all the reds, against which the still impetuous old age of the Pope seems to shine forth still more splendidly.

On 19th March 1546, Titian was invested with the laurel wreath in the Campidoglio, then he left Rome, leaving behind too the 'mannerist crisis.' In 1548 he was in Augusta, at the court of Charles V, of whom he made an equestrian portrait. Soon after, he entered into relations with Philip II and began to send to Madrid numerous paintings, paintings of love, or 'poesie,' that is, inventions or fantasies, and the many portraits, still in the Prado. Around 1555, he painted the wonderful *Martyrdom of St Laurence* for the Venetian Church of the Jesuits. The cruel scene of the burning of the saint takes place during the night in front of the steps of a temple which can be glimpsed through the broken shadows of the flashes of light. The painting is like a clash of fires lit in a sinister way in different places; and from the gash in the clouds another celestial fire descends, bringing other reflections into this incandescent atmosphere. This painting is indeed a triumph of Titian's use of light. At that time, he painted also *St Jerome*, now in the Brera, *Diana and Actaeon*, in London, and the *Annunciation* for the Church of San Salvador in Venice. In this *Annunciation*, the colour seems consumed by the luminous fire which corrodes even the profiles of the bodies within an intense atmospheric density. He also took up his old themes, for example, the *Crowning with Thorns*, now in Monaco, and the *Deposition*, in the Prado. In these works, his imagination has become stronger and more visionary. The violent breaking up of the colours was later to inspire Rembrandt.

In 1574, he wrote to Philip II that he was occupied in painting the *Battle of Lepanto*, and repeated the prayer that he be liquidated of all his belongings. He said he was old and near to death, not only to inspire the court treasurers with pity, but because he really felt he was aged. He died on 27th August 1576 of the plague, and with him his son Ortensio. He was buried the following day in the Frari Church.

Plate 14—LORENZO LOTTO: San Bernardino Altar-piece. The first mention of Lorenzo Lotto is found in a painting of the *Virgin and Child and St Peter Martyr* in Naples Art Gallery. In this painting are the signature and date: L. Lotus 1503. Owing to the strong influence of Giovanni Bellini, this painting is believed to be the earliest of Lotto's works. In later works, this influence gradually disappeared, and Lotto sought for more complex effects. On the basis of this inscription, he must have been born about the year 1480, and although his place of origin has been believed to be Bergamo, in his will, drawn up in 1546, he declared himself to be Venetian, and this Venetian origin was again mentioned when he was accepted as oblate in the Monastery of Loreto in 1554, two years before his death.

Lorenzo Lotto was therefore a contemporary of Titian and Giorgione. He began to paint in

LLOTVS
M D XXI

the years when Venetian painting, from Giovanni Bellini to Giorgione, was beginning to evolve towards a tonal interpretation of Renaissance spatialism. Although, as has been said, he was influenced by Giovanni Bellini, and other works, such as the frescoes of the Onigo monument in the Church of San Niccolò in Treviso, indicate the influence of Antonello, Lotto did not continue along that path, but detached himself firmly from it, even going right away from Venice.

He began to travel at an early age; as a youth, he was already in Recanati; then he went to Treviso, where he painted some altar-pieces, after which he returned to Recanati in 1506, and again went to Venice. In 1509, he was mentioned as being in Rome, while work was being carried out in the Vatican. This restlessness accounts for the different influences which he underwent during his wanderings. Lotto's spiritual unrest was manifested not only in a certain strangeness and instability in his life, but above all in a romantic tension which runs through his works. We have seen the background of Bellini's and Antonello's influence on his painting, but already his original method of placing the figures, and his realistic treatment of narration show that he was beginning to rebel against their teaching.

In 1513 he was in Bergamo, where he painted many works, and especially three large altar-pieces. In the first one, now in the Church of San Bartolomeo, the influence of his journey to Rome can be seen from certain reminiscences of Raphael and of Bramante's architecture; but from the very lively colour and fine details in the narrative we see that he had in addition contact with northern painting, particularly German, and this accentuates the visionary character of Lotto's work. The second work is for the church of Santo Spirito. In this painting the throne of the Virgin is placed in the open, and around it revolves a nimbus of angels. Beautiful in the details, it is however a little slack in composition, perhaps because of its too highly individualistic treatment. The third of these, however, is a masterpiece of sixteenth-century painting. This was painted for the Church of San Bernardino and dated 1521. This work too is exceptional for the invention of the throne placed in the open. Over the throne is spread a large hanging held up by angels, which softens the light and casts reflections of colour and half shadows. From this painting comes the detail of the angel writing at the feet of the Virgin, a wonderfully imaginative touch, to which Lotto gives realism and psychological truth.

Lotto might then have returned to Venice as a master; but he preferred his wandering life. After staying for thirteen years in Bergamo, he returned to the Marches, where in Jesi he painted the screen for the Church of Santa Lucia. From time to time he went to Venice, where he painted a series of portraits which are among the most subtle in the whole of Italian painting. Among them are the *Young Man in the Studio*, now in the Accademia, the *St Nicholas Altar-piece* for the Carmini Church, and the screen painted in 1542, the *Charity of S Antonino*' where Lotto may be said to rival Titian in richness and chromatic splendour. He then continued to wander about the Marches, to Jesi, to Ancona, and to Monte San Giusto, where he left the lively *Crucifixion*.

He was now growing old, and felt tired and in poor health. He obtained shelter in the house of the Oblates at Loreto. He died within two years, leaving to a certain Bartolomeo Carpan four golden scudi, which had been promised to him during Lotto's lifetime.

Plate 15—JACOPO ROBUSTI called TINTORETTO: St Mark Saving a Saracen. Tintoretto was born in 1518 or the following year in Venice, where he passed without interruption the fruitful years of his activity. His nickname, Tintoretto, came to him from the trade of his father, a cloth dyer from Lucca. He died in 1594, the last survival of those great Venetian artists who were his teachers, his colleagues or his competitors; from Titian and Sansovino to Palladio, from Veronese to Bassano and Vittoria; while in Rome, Caravaggio, working in a totally different direction, indicated a new attitude to nature, or naturalism, which led the way to modern painting.

Tintoretto's long period of activity is punctuated by many works, which centre however on the grandiose cycle of paintings for the

Plate 14. LORENZO LOTTO:
San Bernardino Altar-piece. Canvas, 300 x 275 cm. Bergamo, Church of San Bernardino.

Plate 15. JACOPO ROBUSTI called TINTORETTO:
St Mark Saving a Saracen.
Canvas, 416 x 337 cm. Venice, Accademia Gallery.

Plate 16. JACOPO ROBUSTI called TINTORETTO:
The Removal of the Body of St Mark.
Canvas, 421 x 306 cm. Venice, Accademia Gallery.

Scuola Grande di San Rocco. The work on these paintings occupied him, with some interruptions, for more than twenty years (1564-87), and also enabled him to undertake several other commissions of an official character.

If Ridolfi is to be believed, the young Tintoretto was thrown out by Titian after a few days' *apprentissage* in his workshop. This is not surprising, when we think of the difference in feeling and attitude between the two painters, which was to lead Tintoretto to an interesting Tuscan-Roman mannerism by way of the sculpture of Jacopo Sansovino, Pordenone's imitations of Michelangelo, and a study of the models for the statues in the Medici Chapel. His reaction to Titian is apparent above all in the field of his interpretation of colour. Colour was no longer a happy and ample tonal concord for in Tintoretto's painting it freely absorbs the light and almost becomes identical with it, thus creating an impassioned and dramatic atmosphere.

This is, in fact, the inner theme around which gravitates the painting of *St Mark Saving a Saracen*.

The large canvas was, until the beginning of the nineteenth century, part of a cycle of three episodes of the Life of St Mark commissioned in 1562 by the 'Guardian Grande' Tommaso Rangone, a doctor from Ravenna, for the Great Hall of the School of Saint Mark's, to complete the series begun by Tintoretto in 1548 with the *Miracle of the Slave*. In the Accademia Gallery in Venice there is also the *Removal of the Body of St Mark*, while the third canvas, the *Recovery of the Saint's Body*, is now in the Brera in Milan. The cycle was completed in 1566.

The painting represents a miracle of the patron saint of Venice who, during a shipwreck, descended from heaven to save a Saracen who had invoked his aid, and placed him in the boat on which some Venetian merchants had taken refuge. One of these merchants was a portrait of the donor (in the centre of the painting) and he was emphasised by means of his golden robe, just as in the other two canvases. This episode was congenial to the artist's imagination, with the strong drama of the shipwreck and the Saint's intervention from the void to bring salvation.

Tintoretto stressed all the above themes scenically, again using the diagonal composition which was so dear to him, with the apocalyptic swelling of the sea in the tempest, the surging of the waves and the scurrying clouds in the threatening sky. Tintoretto brought dramatic action even to scenes which were tranquil in themselves, such as the *Last Supper*, and found a perfectly adapted instrument in his treatment of colour passing through fillets of light.

Plate 16—JACOPO ROBUSTI called TINTORETTO: The Removal of the Body of St Mark. This work formed part of a cycle representing the Miracles of St Mark, which was painted by Tintoretto for the School of St Mark's.

This painting is quite different in colouring from the painting previously illustrated. In that painting, there dominated the dark sea-green colour of the wild surface of the waves, and the leaden sky, while here instead three cold colours are placed together: the pink of the floor and of some figures, the silver colour of the architecture, lighter on the left and denser on the right, and the tobacco-coloured sky.

But to the novelty of that harsh chromatic dissonance Tintoretto opposed the simple perspective structure of the square. This structure was so simple in its ordered symmetry that it was considered as very archaic (although Titian had been teaching otherwise for many years), and especially was thought to imply two separate operations and a priority of conception. This is overcome by Tintoretto's treatment in which he centres and gathers together every component within the luministic conflict.

If we compare this canvas with the parallel *Miracle* in the Brera, this difference becomes even more evident. By displacing the centre of perspective to the left, Tintoretto has created an asymmetric deformation of space, which ceases to be of interest in itself, and becomes subservient to the spectral atmosphere created by the light.

But, as has been said, the chromatic structure is of prime importance in this painting, of great rarity even within the entire corpus of Tintoretto's works, and may perhaps be a

Plate 17. PAOLO CALIARI called VERONESE: *The Sacrifice of Abraham*. Canvas, 129 x 95 cm. Madrid, Prado.

recollection of the affinity with the silver clear tones of Veronese which Tintoretto showed in his works of around 1555.

The subject itself did not offer great possibilities for brilliance of composition: all that was needed was to recall the tradition, connected with the founding of St Mark's Cathedral, whereby in 828 two merchants, Rustico of Torcello and Buono Tribuno of Malamocco, carried off the body of Saint Mark from Alexandria in Egypt and brought it to Venice. Tintoretto therefore emphasises the historical group of figures on the right, to which, however, he added two others, the 'Guardian Grande' Tommaso Rangone, who commissioned the series, and who is shown supporting the head of the saint, and a portrait of himself on the right. Tintoretto could not fail to create a scene of dramatic vigour. The psychological implications of the act of removing the body are alluded to by the general flight of the bystanders, Tintoretto again insisting on brilliance of gesture rather than on an internal dynamism.

One of the most interesting passages in the painting is the body of the saint, which reveals Tintoretto's interest in Michelangelesque mannerism, which reached him through the sculpture of Jacopo Sansovino, Pordenone's personal interpretation of Michelangelo, and a study of the models for the Medici Chapel statues, which, according to Ridolfi, were those executed by Daniele da Volterra.

The painting is damaged by a large tear on the left, as can be seen by a comparison with early copies and from an engraving by A. Zucchi, now in the Lovisa Collection, and the damage probably occurred in the early nineteenth century, when the work was placed in the Library of St Mark's by the side of the *Miracle of St Mark Saving a Saracen*. As early as 1819, Moschini already noted that the painting was damaged and partly destroyed. From the painting are missing a running man —only the tail of his coat remains to be seen —and a phantasmagorical flying figure—the spirit of Saint Mark.

The canvas was restored in 1960 by Mauro Pellicioli, who brought to light in the cleaning, between the camel and the church, a heap of faggots, which was evidently part of Tintoretto's first sketch, although it is not clear if later artists or Tintoretto himself were responsible for the complete overpainting of the architectonic background.

A drawing for the figure on the left foregr- is to be found in the Spanish Art Gallery in London, according to Tietze, writing in 1944.

Plate 17—PAOLO CALIARI called VERONESE: The Sacrifice of Abraham. In contrast to what was said, or revealed by contemporary documents, on the subject of Titian and Tintoretto, who were both difficult characters, nothing but praise was spoken of Veronese. Ridolfi, in the seventeenth century, said of him: 'He had generous thoughts... He was very frank in his features; he never strove to obtain any position... he always kept his promise and earned praise for every one of his deeds... He lived far from luxuries; he was thrifty in spending.' And Sansovino in 1560, a few years after Veronese arrived at Venice, stated, 'Paolo is beginning to become known as rare in his profession, and also for his gentle manner of conversing and behaving with people.' Written during the years of the somewhat quarrelsome empire of Titian and Tintoretto, these words indicate the great esteem in which the young painter was held. To merit this praise, he had not only accomplished the *Justinian Altar-piece* (1571) on the model of the *Pesaro Altar-piece* of Titian, altar-pieces; but he was completing the decorations for the sacristy and church of San Sebastiano, considered the masterpiece of his early activity in Venice.

Veronese came to Venice from Verona, where he was born in 1528, with an artistic preparation unknown in Venice, owing to the great freedom with which he had been able to conduct the most diverse experiments. He was a pupil of Antonio Badile, as we see from a document of 1541, but looked beyond the teaching of his master. Verona was in a fortunate situation, the meeting place of different provinces and of many new ideas: Brescia with Moretto and Romanino, from which Veronese was to acquire his taste for clear, silvery cold tones; Mantua, with the great monumental and profane works of Giulio Romano; Parma, with the refined elegance of Parmigianino; and without waiting until he had seen other examples in Venice, Titian had sent to Verona itself an *Assumption* to be placed in the Cathedral. To all these influences must be added the influence of Roman art, particularly that of Raphael and Michelangelo. The more clearly we can distinguish these threads of his artistic background, the more we are amazed at the superb faculty of Veronese to effect a synthesis from such diverse cultures. And his painting was not, of course, the sum of purely academic or decorative elements; for he had a prodigious capacity for gathering within himself these different influences and transforming them by his personal vision. In the first place, he acquired a deep feeling for breadth of composition. From Titian and Michelangelo he learned to dominate large figures, to foreshorten the large spaces between which the episodes are rhythmically enacted. With this breadth of composition he was enabled to extend his ample planes of colour, to set against the open skies and monumental perspectives gigantic figures in serpentine and vertical motion. The *Sacrifice of Abraham*, a mature work of the last years of the life of Veronese, reached the Prado from the sacristy of the Escorial, where its presence was mentioned in a document of 1657. This painting demonstrates this breadth of composition and adventurous foreshortening. Within a world of open perspectives, limpid as his own serene temperament, Veronese took every occasion to give resonance to clear colours, in a brilliance without chiaroscuro. The simple spontaneity of his colouring brought him into opposition, at the very moment of his celebrity as a master of Venetian art, to the traditional colouring of Venetian painting—the intellectual and mysterious tonalism of Giorgione, as well as the lively chromatic colouring of Titian.

The innovations introduced by Veronese, in the very heart of Venetian mannerism in the middle of the sixteenth century, were firstly, his very free use of the architecture of the human body, as well as of the sumptuous palaces (we should recall that Sanmicheli, Palladio and Sansovino were his contemporaries); secondly, a new orchestration of colours. The colours were rendered crystalline and sonorous with clear lights, not diluted, but accorded or violently contrasted with the aim of giving prominence to light, yet without breaking it up into dust particles, as in Titian, or, as in Tintoretto, creating dramatic refractions of luminous rays against dark zones.

Plate 18—PAOLO CALIARI called VERONESE: Moses Saved from the Waters. A painting of this subject is mentioned by Ridolfi, the seventeenth century biographer, as being in the house of the Marchese della Torre, in Venice. How it came to Spain is not known; before reaching the Prado it was in the Alcazar in Madrid. On the other hand, Veronese had made various paintings of the same subject, firstly because he liked the worldly and rural aspects of the biblical scene, and secondly because it was a work which met with success, so that he was frequently asked to repeat it; other copies are to be found in the Hermitage Museum in Leningrad and in the museums of Dijon and Lyon.

Just outside the walls of a city, in the calm hour of the afternoon, the wealthy ladies on their walk see the infant floating on the river and take him to the bank. The biblical story has become a scene of the countryside; among the fresh trees the women are clothed in rich garments; the sky is inflamed by the approaching sunset. From every detail, Veronese takes a pretext for using beautiful and magnificent colours and creates a landscape of the neighbouring Venetian countryside of a luminous brilliance. Chronologically, this painting is of the same time as the frescoes painted for the Palladian villa of Maser. This is shown not only by the trees, which replace the perspectives of palaces, portals or monumental arches of the works painted before these frescoes; it is shown especially by the documentation of everyday life, which in the villa Maser is mixed with mythical allegories or witty illusionist *trompe l'œil* and a rich sonority of colour. Hence the date of the work is about 1575, a few years before the death of Veronese, which occurred in 1588 when he was barely sixty years of age.

Veronese boldly placed holy scenes among profane elements, and this brought him a most unwelcome summons to appear before

the Tribunal of the Holy See. In 1573 he completed for the church of SS Giovanni e Paolo the vast canvas depicting the *Supper in the House of the Levites.* The Tribunal imputed to him too much licence, not only in the excessive worldliness and the luxury of the repast, but in certain details: the dogs, the dwarfs or the pages. And with great simplicity, conscious of his rights as an artist, Veronese defended himself before the judges: 'I make paintings with that consideration that is becoming, that my intellect can understand ... We painters take that licence, which is taken by poets and madmen.'

Veronese had previously painted a vast composition of banqueters, the *Marriage at Cana*; this was painted ten years previously for the refectory of the church of San Giorgio Maggiore and is now in the Louvre. This painting did not meet with great success, this time for aesthetic reasons. Veronese himself remarked on the excessive monumental scenography with the inevitably chaotic crowding of the figures, in spite of the fine painting and composition. From then on, there was a progressive thinning of crowds, a growing simplicity, aided by his breadth of composition full of luminous colours, with large figures seen in vertiginous perspectives against skies inundated by a diffused light. And as well as the frescoes of the Maser villa, in which the rich life of the Venetian nobles is depicted with extreme fantasy, these years of Veronese's maturity produced some masterpieces of Venetian art: the organ panel for the church of San Gimignano in Modena, the *Martyrdom of St George* for Verona, the *Allegories*, now in London, the *Family of Darius* also in London, the *Youth with a Greyhound* in New York.

Veronese was a painter of vast luminous compositions where every detail, the gestures of the characters, the clothes, the leaves illuminated like drops of pure colour, marks a moment of joy. But he had too a feeling for scenes of great emotion, and in such paintings as the *Crucifixion* of San Lazzaro, or the *Agony in the Garden* in the Brera, which are influenced by the 'nocturnes' of Bassano, Veronese reveals a note of deep melancholy and sadness, which was the lyrical and creative discovery of the last years of his life.

Plate 19—JACOPO DA PONTE called BASSANO: St Roch Blessing the Pestilent. If Venice was the capital of Venetian art, producing an amazing succession of artists of genius, we should not forget the artists of the provinces, some of them in no way inferior to those of Venice itself. In fact, in the case of Bassano, the fact of being far from Venice with its courtly life, with its constant battles between Titian, Tintoretto and Veronese, enabled him to exercise his talent freely and to take inspiration from diverse sources. For these reasons, Bassano is counted among the greatest masters of his time.

He was born about the year 1515 in Bassano and began in the studio of his father. Then he went to Venice where he worked for a time in the studio of Bonifacio Pitati, until his return home, imbued with the example of Titian and especially of Lotto. He then adopted some of the themes of mannerist painting, which reached him through the works of Pordenone, Tintoretto and Campi. The influence of Dürer is seen in the painting of *Christ and Veronica* in York Museum, but after 1540 it was Parmigianino who exercised a greater influence and Bassano used colour and light in a similar way, to create a fantastic effect, as in the *Adoration of the Shepherds* in Hampton Court, or more noticeably, in the *Beheading of St John Baptist* in the Copenhagen Museum, where the diagonal composition accentuates the brilliance of Bassano's fantasy. At the same time, he preferred subjects where peasant life could be represented with freedom and realism, although with great refinement of colouring and extreme elegance and liveliness of imagination. Certain still lifes in the religious paintings and the strong characterisation anticipate the realism of Spanisart.

After 1560, Bassano found a new theme in his 'nocturnes'. The first of this series is the great *Crucifixion* painted for the church of San Teonisto in Treviso in 1562. If the composition recalls that of Titian's painting in Ancona, the pictorial significance of Bassano's work is entirely different. The charged atmosphere accentuating the drama has an expressionism far removed from naturalistic representation. With his vertical perspectives, with vivid touches of colour lighting up the profiles and the corners of the painting in a

Plate 18. PAOLO CALIARI called VERONESE:
Moses Saved from the Waters.
Canvas, 56 x 43 cm. Madrid, Prado.

Plate 19. JACOPO DA PONTE called BASSANO:
St Roch Blessing The Pestilent.
Canvas, 350 x 210 cm. Milan, Brera Gallery.

play of nocturnal phantoms, Bassano led the way to a form of painting in which the colour itself creates visionary images. El Greco in particular was to be greatly influenced by this, especially in his most sombre and hallucinatory paintings. We see more clearly what constitutes the novelty of Bassano's painting of those years if we compare it with the innovations made by other Venetian painters: Titian, in whose painting the light dissolves in broken patches, or Tintoretto who dynamically breaks up his compositions in flashes of violent chiaroscuro. Bassano, on the other hand, softens the atmosphere and introduces into it vivid flashes of pure colour, which burn like firebrands. Examples of this are the many *Adorations* of those years, the lunette of the *Priors of Vicenza,* the *Baptism of Santa Lucilla* of Bassano Museum, the *Preaching of St Paul* in Marostica, a painting of chromatic brilliance which reveals too a feeling of melancholy peopling the nocturnal darkness of the landscapes deep in shadow with sighs and mysterious figurations.

The St Roch in the Brera is a typical example of this new feeling for chromatic splendour. The colour seems to be alive in itself, although the painting is no less refined and elegant, and the innovation of this painting was to be of major importance to the evolution of seventeenth century art.

Plate 20—GIOVANNI BATTISTA PIAZZETTA: The Soothsayer. Piazzetta was born in Venice in 1682, and began at a very early age to help his father Giacomo, a woodcarver and sculptor. But before he was twenty, he had decided to become a painter and attended the school of Antonio Molinari, although his early work was mainly influenced by luministic painting; in fact, he is usually associated, if indirectly, with Caravaggio.

The painters working in a similar way, who brought Caravaggio's influence to Piazzetta, were the Venetian Antonio Zanchi, a mannerist who emphasised light as the creator of form, and especially the Bolognese artists Giuseppe Maria Crespi and Guercino, with whom he became acquainted during his absence from Venice during the first ten years of the eighteenth century—we have no definite information concerning his whereabouts for the years 1703-11.

The earliest known work of Piazzetta is the Altar-piece of San Filippo Neri, painted for the church of the Filippini in Venice, and concerning which we have a document recording that it was paid for in the year 1727. There then followed some works which show that Piazzetta was occupied, at least until about 1735, in problems of plastic density, of chiaroscuro relief, realised with strong contrasts of light in a mottled effect recalling the earliest works of Guercino. Piazzetta changed his manner between 1735 and 1743 (according to Pallucchini), and where formerly he resolved colour in a scale of warm browns, now he lightened his palette and replaced shadows by blues and transparent skies of atmospheric lightness, thus coming closer to Venetian tradition, especially for his connection with Sebastiano Ricci. Similarly, there entered into his dark plasticity a more subtle and allusive painting with lighter brushstrokes.

The works of Piazzetta's old age contain some elements, such as a darkened chiaroscuro and a return to luministic painting to the detriment of the happy freedom of colour achieved in his middle years, which indicate a falling back upon his initial position, although this was not a complete reversal by any means. Of this time were the many splendid drawings (many of which were made for prints or book illustrations) which caused Fiocco unhesitatingly to declare Piazzetta 'the greatest draughtsman of the eighteenth century'. But the painter, whose studio had formerly been much frequented, reduced his activity considerably in the last years of his life, and although he was nominated in 1750 to be Director of the Venice Accademia, he died in solitary yet dignified poverty.

The *Soothsayer* was bought for the Accademia Gallery in Venice in 1886. It is perhaps the most famous work of Piazzetta, and is traditionally considered to be one of his finest paintings. On the back of the painting is the inscription 'Sepulchral inscription of the Famous Painter Piazzetta Author of this Painting commissioned from him in Venice in 1740 and paid for fifteen Zecchini...'

Piazzetta is not interested in realism. The characters are arranged around the female

Plate 20. GIOVANNI BATTISTA PIAZZETTA: *The Soothsayer.* Canvas, 154 x 114 cm. Venice, Accademia Gallery.

Plate 21. GIOVANNI BATTISTA TIEPOLO: *Meeting of Anthony and Cleopatra.* Fresco. Venice, Palazzo Labia.

protagonist on the left, who plays with the lapdog held by the soothsayer under her arm, while on the right are two hens in front of a peasant and a youth, in a spatial composition with diagonal axis which aims directly and exclusively at effects of light; the scenic architecture has become resolved into an architecture of 'solid light', as a contemporary has defined it.

The colour sparkles in the modulations and folds of the protagonist's dress, with rapid and concise brushstrokes of delicate tones. The corsage is dove-pink, the skirt violet-pink against darker tones. But there are also contrasts of light and shade which give strength to the painting: the beautiful passage of the profile in shadow against the inundation of light filtering between the two female figures; the other contrast of the two men. However, the felicity and ease of Piazzetta's manner of painting reveal, as Longhi has justly remarked, that the similarity with Caravaggio is no more than apparent.

Plate 21—GIOVANNI BATTISTA TIEPOLO: Meeting of Anthony and Cleopatra. The Labia Palace was begun around the year 1720 and completed thirty years later; the façade facing San Geremia is by the architect Tremignan, while the richer façade facing Cannareggio is by Andrea Cominetti. Tiepolo was entrusted with the decoration of the main hall. He began the work about 1745 and finished it in 1750, that is, shortly after his departure for Germany, where he was summoned to decorate the residential bishop's palace in Würzburg. This painting is therefore a mature work of Tiepolo's prodigiously inventive and elegant art. While his collaborator Girolamo Mengozzi-Colonna prepared the solemn scenographic perspectives of the false architecture, Tiepolo painted the vast frescoes, on one side the scene of the *Meeting of Anthony and Cleopatra*, and on the other the scene of *Cleopatra's Banquet*, where the queen is shown in the act of dissolving a pearl in a goblet of wine.

This is the most complex and sumptuous series of paintings which Tiepolo executed for a private palace in Venice. At that time, the seventeenth century crisis in Venetian painting had long been overcome, and Tiepolo could follow the example of Titian and Veronese without for that reason restraining his own creative fantasy.

Many decades had now transpired since Tiepolo's early works. He was nineteen when in 1715 he painted the *Sacrifice of Isaac* for the church of the Ospedaletto. In this painting it can be seen that Tiepolo had looked closely at the work of Sebastiano Ricci and Piazzetta, who were working in a tradition opposed to the 17th century Venetian academic style. Perhaps as a reaction to this academic tradition, and also because of the fresh outlook of his youth, the first paintings of Tiepolo are dense with red shadows, corporeal volumes, excited gestures and lighted lamps. In these works, rather than a real dramatic sense, is a taste for theatrical effect, for complex and lively scenes. The *Martyrdom of St Bartholomew*, which was painted about 1720 for the Church of San Stae, is, in spite of the cruel instruments of torture, more like a ballet than a scene of torture. But its main importance lies in the lively movement which, as in Piazzetta, rejects the immobile eloquence of the seventeenth century manner.

The typical clear atmosphere of Tiepolo's paintings, impregnated with sparkling light and white clouds, with figures of rosy coloured flesh, does not appear until later, when in 1726 he was sent for in order to decorate the Bishop's Palace in Udine. This work recalls Veronese, but with a more airy vastness and a greater sharpness and lightness in design, which is light as the air palpitating through his landscapes. The success which immediately came to him caused him to be summoned from Venice to Milan to decorate the Archinto and Casati-Dugnani Palace, to Bergamo for the Colleoni Chapel, and again to Milan in 1740 for the ceiling decoration of the Clerici Palace, where in the scene of the sun chariot and the sea gods there emerges a fantasy and pictorial brilliance of great vivacity. Painting was, for Tiepolo, the means to conquering the airy and fantastic spaces dear to the Baroque ideal. He opened up immense skies with illusionary luminosity. And within these open spaces, or in contrast to them, he gathered everyday characters, mythological beings, allegorical or literary incarnations, and brought them together in one reality: a reality of lyrical opera rather than tragedy. For Tiepolo never felt the weight or grief of the drama, and even where the scene of the martyrdom becomes most cruel, it merely serves him with a pretext for gathering crowds, waving standards, for flashes of light and brilliantly coloured cloaks. He displayed a lively exuberance which weighed down his compositions yet always aimed at chromatic effect, at gathering and imprisoning light.

After completing the ceiling of the Ca' Pisani in Stra, Tiepolo left for the court of Madrid, where he painted the frescoes on the ceiling of the royal palace. He died on 27th March, 1770, at a time when his painting was beginning to undergo the adverse criticism of the rising neo-classicists.

Plate 22—ANTONIO CANAL called CANALETTO: The Return of the Bucintoro. Canaletto was born in Venice in 1697 and died there in 1769. He began to paint in collaboration with his father Bernardo, who painted for the theatre, and we know with certainty that between 1716 and 1719 he participated in painting the scenery in Venetian theatres for the productions of Antonio Vivaldi and other composers. But in 1719, tired of the pretensions of dramatists, as Zanetti relates, Canaletto entered the studio of the 'vedutista' Carlevaris, and then went to Rome, at his suggestion, evidently with the ambition of moving from the mechanics of painting theatrical scenery to a greater individuality. He certainly continued to paint within the framework of his earliest activity, by dedicating himself almost exclusively to 'views' which were much sought after by foreign visitors. Yet he completely avoided yielding to a painting of the documentary type of Caspar van Wittel or Pannini, whose work he saw in Rome. He was able to achieve a literal and impersonal transcription of the subject, by means of the camera obscura, and a great precision and exactness of vision. We know too, from a correspondence of 1725-6 with the Luccan Stefano Conti which has been recently published, and also from the Sketchbook in the Accademia Gallery in Venice, that Canaletto worked on the spot. This was another important indication of his will to overcome the mechanical painting of the old perspective tradition, and this attitude was not only new, it was also modern. The light became a means of fixing spatial relations and transferring the object on to the plane of poetry.

From the time of his earliest works, the paintings executed for the Conti, now in Montreal, and the others painted in 1728 for the Duke of Richmond, Canaletto based his activity on the 'views' large numbers of which remain, especially in the Liechtenstein Collection, in the Dresden Art Gallery, the National Gallery London and in the Grenoble Museum.

Another important stage in his work is indicated by a series of five views of ancient Roman monuments in Windsor Castle, dated and signed 'Ant. Canal fecit Anno MDCCXLII,' and the famous *Colosseum* in Hampton Court, signed and dated the following year. These paintings led to the belief that Canaletto took a second journey to Rome about the year 1740, and they open the way to a calmer style of painting, after the liveliness of the earlier chiaroscuro, with a more diffused light, in the tradition of Venetian art.

Canaletto stayed in London from 1746 to 1755, apart from a brief interruption in 1751. The English works have a more meticulous style, a more terse luminosity and greater transparency of tones. This may have been due to the influence of Flemish painting which Canaletto saw in England. Yet the fact that these qualities were already present in the early Venetian works immediately preceding his departure for England diminishes the validity of this argument.

In his last works, Canaletto painted in a more easy manner, with a freedom and lightness which may perhaps not have been immune to the influence of Guardi.

The *Return of the Bucintoro* was executed immediately prior to the works dated 1742 and 1743, that is, it is a work of the best period of Canaletto's activity. The perspective is of a sound mathematical rigour, with exact modulations of tones and precisely rendered dark shadows. In this painting is to be found an exactitude and seriousness which, when compared with the usual approximations, provides

Plate 22. ANTONIO CANAL called CANALETTO:
The Return of the Bucintoro. Canvas, 139 x 187 cm. Milan, Mario Crespi Collection.

Plate 23. FRANCESCO GUARDI:
Gala Concert. Canvas, 69 x 91 cm. Munich Art Gallery.

a reconstruction of the data of nature on a rational basis.

Plate 23 — FRANCESCO GUARDI: Gala Concert. Francesco Guardi came from a family of painters. In the family studio worked his father Domenico, his brothers Gian Antonio and Niccolò, a sister and his son Giacomo. From the time of his birth, in 1712, he may be said to have had a paint-brush between his fingers. It may be thought that it was from his brother, who had become head of the studio, that he first learned to paint. But as he was a boy of talent, he watched what was taking place beyond the circle of his own house; and looking at his works, we can see which masters he studied: Maffei and Bazzani of the previous century, Ricci, Magnasco and Pellegrini among his contemporaries, all painters gifted with a lively capacity for an imaginative representation of reality.

The works produced in the studio were not of great importance. Most often they were copies of paintings of the sixteenth and seventeenth centuries, as we see from the will of Count Giovanni Benedetto Giovanelli, or religious paintings for minor or provincial churches. These were therefore only the works on which Guardi practised his art. Yet they did not spoil the hand of the young artist, and in fact he achieved a few successes, which are now seen to be pictorial innovations, but were then considered little less than extravagances: the painting for the chapel of Cerete Basso in the valley around Bergamo, done in collaboration with Gian Antonio, and the organ panel for the church of the Archangel Raphael, Venice, depicting the *Life of Tobias*. This is a lively painting, which seems to sparkle as if reflected in cut diamonds. The rapid brushstrokes accentuate the mobile and instantaneous appearance of the figures within a cold and transparent atmosphere, vaporous with drops of colour or marbled reflections. In spite of the delightful novelty of Guardi's painting, which contains all the grace and brilliance of extreme Rococo art, he was not greatly acclaimed in his lifetime. Only in the last ten years of his life, which ended on 10th January 1793, was he admitted as a member of the Academy of Painting and Sculpture—and even then there were some dissenting votes.

We cannot say precisely when Guardi began to paint views, and if he was impelled to do so by a desire of his own or by a necessity of the studio to sell paintings which were very much in request by the fashion of the time. It is probable that for these paintings he worked with Marieschi, but he must soon have formed a style of his own, as during the absence of Canaletto from Venice between 1751 and 1755, and particularly after his death in 1768, Guardi was among the best of the Venetian 'vedutisti'. In these works, his fantasy was extended with a liberty unknown in Venetian painting. An examination of his landscapes, his 'fantasies', his often imaginary reconstructions of countries and ruins, show that he did not ignore the troubled painting of Magnasco, the rapid brushstrokes of Ricci; but the effects of absolute brilliance came only from his own hand, guided by the emotion of his fantastic vision. He soon surpassed the lucid clear-cut perspective of Canaletto, the luminous but impassive airiness of Carlevaris, and he translated the Venetian 'view' into a work of fresh and brilliant fantasy. If Canaletto offered a document of Venetian urban life, Guardi offers an evocation of that life through a sparkling light which deforms and accentuates perspective, producing a magical effect, and inflaming the whole atmosphere with a fire which corrodes the profiles, consumes the chromatic masses, in dazzling brilliance. As Canaletto before him, Guardi too found fortune and esteem with an English collector, John Strange. His collection, which was sold in 1799, contained many 'vedute' acquired directly from Guardi.

The *Gala Concert* was painted in 1782, to record a visit made by the Russian Archduke Paolo Petrowitz with Maria Teodorovna. Six canvases were ordered by the Venetian Republic to record these festivities, but only four have reached us, among them this concert of ladies.

Plate 24—PIETRO LONGHI: The Morning of a Venetian Lady. Longhi was born in Venice in 1702 and died there in 1785. He began to paint in the studio of Antonio Balestra, an academic painter, but in Bologna he frequented Giuseppe Maria Crespi and worked in his studio, and this influence was far more fruitful.

Longhi began painting in the traditional manner, as we see, unhappily, from his famous fresco of the *Giants* in the Palazzo Sagredo, which he painted about 1734. He then dedicated himself almost exclusively to the small bourgeois scenes for which he is famous, although in his own time he was particularly renowned as a portrait painter. Longhi can therefore, although only approximately, be placed beside the view painters, not only because of the small format of the paintings which destined them for domestic decoration, but above all for their stamp of truth in the documentation of the life of his city. His outlook was decidedly modern, especially when compared with Piazzetta and the slightly older Tiepolo, the last of the great decorative painters of the seventeenth century.

Longhi's interest in reality undoubtedly found precedents in Crespi, whose influence is reflected particularly in the series of the *Sacraments*, which can be dated after 1750, and above all, as Roberto Longhi has recently pointed out, '... in the bourgeois and popular painting of Brescia and Bergamo, which with Ghislandi and Ceruti at the end of the seventeenth and beginning of the 18th century, was the most serious and sincere painting produced in the Venetian republic.'

It should not be forgotten that Ceruti had not only worked in nearby Padua, but that in Venice itself he had left the frescoes of the large staircase in the Palazzo Grassi, which have recently and justly been restituted to him, as a fine example of precise documentation of Venetian life, although of a social class which did not particularly interest him.

Pietro Longhi does not show the firmness of presentation which appears in the ' squalids ' of Ceruti, piteously cruel in their stark simplicity. Longhi prefers a linking of characters through the narrative, within a historical framework, but the richness of the costumes often fail to hide a profound melancholy.

Venetian bourgeois life appears in this *toilette* of the Accademia Gallery in Venice, a work believed to be of the same period as the *Concert* in the same museum, dated 1741. These are therefore among the earliest of Longhi's works of this type.

This painting could superficially be read as a historical document, containing however hints of a class polemic which reaches a vast negative judgment of a society at its decline. One could limit oneself to praising its richness of colour, its refined delicacy of tones.

Instead the most intimate and authentic message of Longhi appears elsewhere: in the caustic definition of character. The chambermaid who holds the mirror is a portrait of subtle melancholy, while the old woman carrying the coffee is a stupendous passage of such precision that we suspect it to be a portrait from life.

The characters transcend the gestures which compose them on the scene in an at least apparent narrative unity. They are isolated, placed in a suspended and enchanted atmosphere, outside time, and only the softness of the colour and the tenderness of painting benevolently, almost piteously, replace them within the circle of normality and re-attach them to life.

So the famous knowledge and industry of Longhi are seen to be more than professional skill. The agility and evanescence of the brushstrokes suggest appearances of men and things, punctuating, underlining and distending wider chromatic zones, thus revealing not only the liberty of a modern outlook but a conscience and will of a most unequivocal firmness, even where it would seem most to be diluted.

Plate 24. PIETRO LONGHI:
The Morning of a Venetian Lady. Canvas, 39 x 47 cm. Venice, Accademia Gallery.

FM2.5 1.42.58.